"All around the church, peopl his inspired, helpful guidan joins with Kara Root to give and pastoral leadership, an exte... by a vibrant faith in a living, active God. In an age when so much about our world, our children, our families, and our church is out of our control, Andy and Kara show us how to live as pastors, parents, and Christians with grace, conviction, and assurance that God is yet with us. A wonderfully inspiring, immediately helpful book."

—**Will Willimon**, author of *Accidental Preacher: A Memoir*;
Duke Divinity School; United Methodist bishop, retired

"*A Pilgrimage into Letting Go* is a gentle, unflinching companion for anxious parents and worn-out church leaders. With honesty, depth, and just the right amount of humor, Andy and Kara Root remind us of what we keep forgetting: we were never in control anyway. This isn't another book of parenting hacks or pastoral tricks—it's a soulful invitation to walk with trust, to make peace with uncertainty, and to recognize and name the presence of God in the midst of it all."

—**Amanda Hontz Drury**, Indiana Wesleyan University

"With wisdom forged in the tensions of parenting, pastoring, and pilgrimage, Andrew and Kara Root offer a profound meditation on the spiritual necessity of surrender. Drawing on deep theological insight and lived experience, they uncover the illusions of control that shape our modern anxieties, and they invite us instead into the liberating posture of trust, resonance, and true presence. This book is a gift to all who seek to walk with God in the uncontrollable terrain of real life."

—**John Swinton**, University of Aberdeen; author of *Finding Jesus in the Storm: The Spiritual Lives of Christians with Mental Health Challenges*

"Our contemporary age is obsessed with the desire to control the world around us. For safety concerns. For health reasons. Out of economic necessity. Because we have the technological means to get hold of social and physical processes. But life is essentially uncontrollable. Only if we accept that, if we learn the art of letting go, will we find what we are looking for. This is the lesson Andrew and Kara Root teach us in this delicately woven, wonderfully written, and truly eye-opening book."

—**Hartmut Rosa**, Friedrich Schiller University

A PILGRIMAGE INTO LETTING GO

helping parents and pastors
embrace the uncontrollable

Andrew Root
and Kara K. Root

BrazosPress

a division of Baker Publishing Group
Grand Rapids, Michigan

Published by Brazos Press
a division of Baker Publishing Group
Grand Rapids, Michigan
BrazosPress.com

Printed in the United States of America

Library of Congress Cataloging-in-Publication Data
Names: Root, Andrew, 1974– author | Root, Kara K. author
Title: A pilgrimage into letting go : helping parents and pastors embrace the uncontrollable / Andrew Root and Kara K. Root.
Description: Grand Rapids, Michigan : Brazos Press, a division of Baker Publishing Group, [2025]
Identifiers: LCCN 2025003647 | ISBN 9781587436628 paperback | ISBN 9781587436840 casebound | ISBN 9781493452156 ebook
Subjects: LCSH: Parenting—Religious aspects—Christianity | Control (Psychology)—Religious aspects—Christianity | Child rearing—Religious aspects—Christianity
Classification: LCC BV4529 .R66 2025 | DDC 248.8/45—dc23/eng/20250318
LC record available at https://lccn.loc.gov/2025003647

Stories told in this book reflect the authors' present recollections of experiences over time. Some names and characteristics have been changed, some events have been compressed, and some dialogue has been re-created.

Cover illustration by Becca Thorne / IllustrationX
Art direction by Paula Gibson

25 26 27 28 29 30 31   7 6 5 4 3 2 1

To Owen and Maisy,
who walked each step with us,
and with whom we promise to walk each coming step—
whether those steps involve meeting saints
or confronting monsters.
Your lives are our greatest joy.

Contents

St. Cuthbert's Way

SCOTTISH BORDERS

NORTHUMBERLAND

MELROSE
Melrose Abbey
St. Boswells
Eildon Hills 422m
KELSO
Dryburgh Abbey
Harestanes Visitor Centre
JEDBURGH
Jedburgh Abbey
Cessford Castle
Town Yetholm
Morebattle
Wideopen Hill 368m
WOOLER
St. Cuthbert's Cave
Lindisfarne Abbey
Fenwick
HOLY ISLAND
A1

Courtesy of the Scottish Borders Council, with adaptations

Acknowledgments

Huge thanks to the brilliant and insightful collection of fellow church leaders, parents, and readers of Rosa: Blair and Vivian Bertrand, Arlene Flancher, Nancy Lee Gauche, Pat Morrison, Kelly Soifer, and Rachel Farris, who graciously read an early draft and gave invaluable feedback. Your responses made this book so much clearer, deeper, more accessible, and more enjoyable. Thank you to Mike King and Youthfront for the privilege of working on the Presence-Centered Parenting project, which was a forum to hone some of these ideas, particularly the theological elements of parenting and of churches centering children. Thank you to David Wood, with whom Andy has partnered in the Relevance to Resonance project, and that project's reading of Rosa. Both projects were funded by the Lilly Endowment, with the initiatives shepherded by Jessicah Duckworth. Thanks for believing in our work. Finally, we'd like to thank the team at Baker, particularly Bob Hosack and Eric Salo for their belief and investment in this book, and Jeremy Wells and Paula Gibson for their care in the design and presentation.

1

Control-Freak Parenting

Slow and Steady

As we squish our bare, cold feet through the final hundred yards of wet sand along the receded sea—the water pulling itself back like a curtain of welcome—our hearts swirl with a potent mix of gratitude and the uncomfortable sense of yielding. Something inside us is changing right now. The withdrawn sea has left wide puddles and strips of seaweed as beacons leading us onward to the shore of Lindisfarne, also known as the Holy Island. It all feels like a miracle—not only that the sea recedes for our arrival but that we made it this far at all. We are approaching the conclusion of a seven-day, ostensibly 100-kilometer (63.5-mile) spiritual walk through the Borderlands between Scotland and England with our teenaged kids. Of course, this receding sea happens every day on this island off the coast of Northumberland, England, regardless of who is nearby. But we are completing an ancient pilgrimage to the

Holy Island on this singular day—and on this day at least, the sea recedes just for us pilgrims.

Lindisfarne is accessible only when the tide is out. Without a boat, it is reachable only two ways: either by foot on the pilgrim's way across the mudflats or by vehicle on the causeway. We walk three miles across the soggy mudflats, the rain stinging our faces and every aching step announcing itself in our sore ankles as our feet press into the mud. Meanwhile, cars and buses stream across the smooth causeway with speed and ease. They are filled with tourists coming to the island for a quick look at the castle and abbey, a little shopping, some ice cream and trinkets. They are all hurried. They must be. They need to return before the afternoon tide rises and covers over their escape route on the causeway.

But not us. We go slow and steady, pressing into the wind, mile sixty-one. Sixty-two. Sixty-three. We're on a quest, and this journey is changing us.

Control-Freak Parenting

We're both control freaks. Though this need for control makes us anxious, we nevertheless seek it relentlessly. We moderns use control as our primary strategy to feel secure, reduce anxiety, combat fear, and give us a feeling of protection and worth. Tense with the need for control, we still seem to believe that the only cure for the stress of needing control is, oddly, more control. It's a circle we've both run very well. We've both been culturally rewarded for effectively sprinting this circle. We're both firstborn, white, middle-class Americans raised at the end of the twentieth century. Control is our bread and butter. Growing up, we sought control with our younger siblings, and in each of our large church youth groups we were handed a good deal of control and told at a young age that we were leaders. All this made us ready to *be* leaders, fast-tracking us from university to seminary, into ordination and a PhD program, to a solo pastorate and a professorship.

But this anxiety over the need for control medicated with more control did *not* prepare us for parenthood. Nineteen years into our parenting pilgrimage, it's fair to say we've been decent parents. Maybe even good ones at times. But as firstborn youth-group stars, we were told that we were made for something *great* (as if that can be controlled). We've been decent parents, good enough parents. But often, usually unknowingly, we've believed that the best and *right* way to parent is to seek control. We've tried to control our kids' choices and behaviors toward what we think is right. Or if we can't control *them*, we control all the contingencies they might face. We've let fear—fear of loss, fear of failure, fear of pain—determine our parenting more than we'd like to admit. Even this discussion itself, this assessing and comparing (*Are we good parents? How good? How do we know if we're good enough?*), is a sign of the howling fear and anxiety under the surface of modern existence, an anxiety that we seek to navigate and smother with our myriad strategies of control.

Until now, we would never have overtly *said* that our goal is to control our kids or that it's good to be controlling. Of course not. We don't really believe that, or at least we don't *want* to believe that. But that has certainly been our default way of functioning. Control as a *good thing* has been assumed by us and by the larger, middle-class, Western society around us. It's become so prevalent in modern parenting that helicopter parenting has given way to snowplow parenting: preparing the road of life for our kids rather than preparing our kids for the road of life. According to cultural theorist Greg Lukianoff and social psychologist Jonathan Haidt, we're operating with some modern "untruths": that adversity leads to fragility (rather than resilience), that emotional beliefs are always true, and that people are either "good" or "bad."[1] This makes parenting a fearful task indeed, driving us to try to shape what our kids will encounter. We think it is our job as parents to protect our children from adversity, sad feelings, and bad people. This (futile) task requires a staggering amount of control. In both large and small ways, we know we have absorbed this logic in our parenting. We've behaved as though it is best to control. And if we had been granted children who were accommodating to our control, we might be writing a much different book. It would likely be an obnoxious book filled with bullet points of pithy wisdom and parenting insights wrapped in cute stories that would undoubtedly make you feel the way you do about your yoga instructor—that you could never have control like they do.

But we can't do that because our own attempts at control met the will of our oldest child. Our son, a firstborn child being raised by two firstborns, and a private, introverted kid at that—God bless the boy!—would have none of it. He would not be controlled. Our late-modern parental reflex to mitigate our kids' discomfort, prevent their pain, monitor what they're exposed to, give them resources, pad their college apps, and broaden their horizons (but not so much that they might get hurt) reveals that we've been more interested in preparing the road for our children than preparing our children for the road. Parenting today feels like a taut balancing act of maximizing opportunities while minimizing risk, and this requires a whole lot of control, or at least the illusion of it.

Through many fights and failures, we've come to see that parenting is fundamentally uncontrollable. Dare we say, parenting is preparing our kids for the path that will—without doubt—lead to death. All lifetimes end in the uncontrollable moment of passing from bodily being to not being. On this pathway of life, no matter how much control we attain or wield, death is the great uncontrollability toward which every life leads. *Nothing* we do can make this untrue.

4

Youth-Group Stars Save the Church

In both of our day-to-day lives and livelihoods, we are walking this path not only as parents but also as leaders in the church. And so, we're carrying a lot of baggage. We're of a generation of youth-group stars who function like firstborn children to American Protestantism. With our modern, control-minded sensibility, it's assumed the church's health, vitality, and even future existence depends on our individual intentionality. Imagine that! It's easy to slip into unreflectively believing that the church is weak, like a vulnerable infant. Perhaps it's more accurate to say the church is seen as a fragile, slow, elderly great-grandmother who is losing her grip on the world around her. How easy it is for us modern church leaders to behave as though the church is our dependent, rather than our own parent and guide.

The two of us have been told for decades that the church is about to die, and the message began when we were young, with the assertion that only we youth-group stars could save it. We can still remember hearing those impassioned sermons in sprawling conference halls alongside other breathless, earnest young people. How natural it was to slip into believing that we were called to parent the church instead of allowing the church to parent us. The church needed us! It was too out of touch, too unstable, too irrelevant, too broken to carry on for long without us, let alone to guide or direct us.

We forgot—or maybe as Protestants we never knew—that the church is our own mother, and until the kingdom comes in its fullness, the church is fit to hold us in her uncontrollable embrace. We were taught that the church was a helpless thing we needed to take control of and lead. You can see it all over X (Twitter) and Facebook (and Threads, or whatever the latest new thing is): Many of us former Protestant youth-group stars, now grown and middle-aged, have this tendency to think that we know better than the church. That our parent—the church—is not fit to raise us or to be trusted with our own children. Without us to mediate her message and redirect her approach, won't she inflict damage—with all her outdated theories and methods? Without irony or humility, we assume that we children must take control of the life of the parent, though we may be ignorant or utterly unconcerned about the deeper life, ritual, and tradition that the church has lived. This is more than a little infantilizing.

To be clear, the church is not pure or without fault. From the crusades and the Inquisition to televised prosperity gospel revivals and sex abuse scandals, the church's culpability is empirically provable. But our response to the big and small failures has created an overwhelming propensity to take control. We might even assume that what is wrong with the church, both morally and structurally, is a lack of control—at least the *right kind* of control. If we don't *do something*, and quickly, the church, like our elderly great-grandmother, will slide into complete irrelevance and die. The church is in danger of hurting herself and, shamefully, many others. We must take away the keys, forbid her from driving at night.

Oddly—and predictably—we've responded to the church's well-documented misuses of power by taking control. This leads us to think that even decline can be beaten by using the tools of capitalist control—innovation, optimization, political-ideological pursuits, and more. Out of our anxiety, we former youth-group-star types have worked hard to *control* the church to medicate our own anxiety *about* the church.[2]

The anxiety of decline produces a more acute desire for control, working us harder and faster, which only generates more anxiety, pushing us to (near) burnout. The terrifying threat of—and seemingly inescapable barreling toward—burnout produces resentment in us. But this steep pitch toward resentment is aimed not toward our desire to seek control but toward the church itself! So we tell ourselves the church needs to change. The church is burning people out. We need to change the church! And the push for control continues.

The Centrality of Control

As modern people, we've accepted without question that control is the mechanism that brings stability and security. Chaos is kept at bay by the firm grasp of control in myriad ways we take for granted: streetlights, paved roads, houses in close proximity, and FDA oversight of the prepacked vegetables lining our temperature-controlled grocery store refrigerator cases. We don't have to worry about being mauled by a wild animal on our way home from our in-laws or losing multiple children to food-borne illnesses. People are not meant to live in chaos. Because control has brought a baseline of order and safety—and resultant goods—to our daily lives, when chaos comes, we are thrust into existential terror. The utter vulnerability—both practically and existentially—of things being out of control can overwhelm us.

When Kara was a hospital chaplain in her early twenties, she encountered this reality inside herself. She could easily be present to the older woman needing a hip replacement and the middle-aged, sedentary man who had suffered a heart attack. But the cancer floor filled her with dread. Particularly, encountering younger people just stepping into adulthood who were now dying from cancer paralyzed her in fear. Cancer is not contagious, but vulnerability is. Uncontrollability feels extremely contagious. We can't blame people who have cancer, but we wish we could. When someone's "control" has been taken away, it reveals how out of control all of us human beings actually are.

A calculated murder or heated argument that results in someone being shot feels entirely different from a middle-school shooting or someone opening fire on a parade or in a restaurant. The randomness of the event—the possibility that random horror happens all the time, and that we can't control it—destabilizes us.

The global pandemic exposed our desperation for control on a grand scale. When the chaos of an unpredictable virus crashed upon us, and our daily patterns and (worldwide) predictable mechanisms of reliable order vanished abruptly, many of us felt a panicked need for some kind of road map or timeframe. We told ourselves we could cope with the shutdowns and disruptions *if we could just get an end date.* "When will this be over?" we thought (or shouted) in frustration. "Just tell me when we'll be finished with this!" We were mad (and anger led some of us to assume someone was hiding something) because no one could control it, and therefore no one could give us an end date. That just made us angrier because we yearned for some control, or for *someone* to be in control. If the CDC or WHO could have just said, "The pandemic will be over on May 15, 2021," we could cope, plan, and pacify our anxiety with some semblance of control. Instead we rode the uncontrollable waves, whether we wanted to or not.

Smooth sailing is the *expected* norm (despite it not being the *experienced* norm). In the storm, when the terrible diagnosis or the job loss hits, in times of prolonged financial instability or extended physical or mental suffering of ourselves or loved ones, we seek control as our salvation. Life's struggles become a problem to be fixed, a malfunction to be corrected. Rather than navigate the darkness by the stars, survive the tumult by shutting off the engines and riding the waves, or steer ourselves by listening and responding to the direction of the wind, we seek to silence the storm, stifle the suffering (or at least navigate it with highly advanced technology and endless information and data), and solve the crisis as quickly and definitively as possible. To keep our own existential terror at bay, we seek to

8

regain (our illusion of) control. To keep ourselves on course and our desired future in sight, we tell ourselves we must maintain control. To say it another way, when control is our fearfully gripped hammer, everything becomes a nail.

Parenting and Church Leadership as Control?

All modern forms of leadership are susceptible to the temptation to find validation through control. Parenting and church leadership have this in common. The best parents and the best church leaders are assumed to be those who take control. Whether heavy-handed or light, control, it's presumed, is needed. We all know from the plentiful examples of dictators and authoritarians that, taken too far, control is dangerous, yet our cultural location inside late modernity has often kept us from questioning control. What else is a leader to do?

This book explores our assumptions about control. Rather than grasping for control, we've come to believe that there is a more fundamental and faithful way of living and leading that connects us to our humanity and each other and attunes us to what God is—and has always been—doing in the world (even in and through the church). Against the backdrop of our own week-long pilgrimage, walking St. Cuthbert's Way with our kids, we examine the journeys of both parenting and pastoring through the life of St. Cuthbert and the thought of contemporary German social theorist Hartmut Rosa. Rosa directly addresses the futility of our modern use of control in his little book *The Uncontrollability of the World*, which will serve as a dialogue partner in this project.

Rosa has been the leading global thinker on how human beings engage the world and why many of our late-modern ways of engagement, and therefore concepts of the "good life," are paralyzing, acidic, and destructive. *The Uncontrollability of the World* is one of Rosa's shortest but, in our minds, most important books. Its importance rests in its moral, and even theological, significance—something fascinating to witness in a social theorist. He explores how most of our so-called best practices for acting and living in the world lead us into *disconnection* from the world rather than *connection* with the world. This disconnection makes us depressed instead of enlivened.

Acceleration and Alienation

Some stage setting will help us understand why control has become so central a tool in modern life, parenting, and leadership. In Rosa's entire body of work, he discusses at length both the poison (which he calls "social acceleration") and its antidote (which he calls "resonance"). Rosa's first books describe the poison of acceleration. Every part of our lives is going faster and faster. Modernity, the modern project, is fundamentally about controlling our relationship with time. And there is no better way to control time than to commodify it. Benjamin Franklin saw this at the beginning of the modern period when he said, "Time is money."[3] Because time is money, time must be accelerated so that it, like money, can be grown and expanded, used and not wasted, giving us more and more reach into the world.

But reaching into the world by the force of acceleration does not end up giving us more connection to the world. Rather, it alienates us from the world. When time is money, the need to procure more and more becomes everything. Everything becomes an object to possess and control. Rather than being full of meaning, time becomes hollow and rushed, keeping us from ever resting in the moment or being still in the now. Our attention is on what is *coming*, what *could be*, what is *next*. Though we are alive right now in time, we come to feel alienated from our very lives inside time. Rosa says, "Alienation denotes a relation of relationlessness in which subject and world find themselves inwardly unconnected from, indifferent toward, and even hostile to each other."[4] Life is moving too fast, accelerating too quickly, for us to feel like we're really living. We become disconnected from, indifferent to, even hostile toward our day-to-day existence. We begin to imagine that it's only on the weekends or on vacation or in retirement that our real living will happen. Because it is only in *those* circumstances that we can let go and simply be in time, playing in time instead of time playing us.

Why Slowing Down Won't Really Help

In modernity, the weekend, vacation, and retirement are when time takes a break from being about the reach for more money and growth. We give the weekend, vacation, and retirement such important weight in our lives, longing for them deeply, because we believe we can slow down only then, when we are allowed to be in time differently. When we live for the breaks, our lives become all about getting to those breaks. Retirement becomes the ultimate break, because now at sixty-five (or is it seventy-two? or eighty?) we'll supposedly get to cash in all the time we've spent growing our money or building our careers and just live in the slowdown of the eternal weekend, the forever vacation.

But you get to this never-ending vacation only by having *used* your time well, accelerating fast enough to have grown your money to a point that you can now live off the illusion of your money's perpetual expanse. The only way to achieve this slowdown of the weekend, vacation, or retirement is through a lot of hard and fast work, as Loverboy pointed out way back in their 1981 song, "Everybody's working for the weekend." To reiterate: *In modernity, slowing down must be worked for.* The reward for winning the speed game of acceleration is the right to slow down. This paradoxical nonsense reveals slowing down as impotent medicine for the ailment of acceleration, because our slowing down itself exists inside the very logic of acceleration. Our *actual experiences* of the weekend, vacation, or retirement reveal that simply trying to slow down is a feeble solution, too frail to stand up against the riptide of acceleration. During these times in which we are supposedly free to slow down, acceleration nevertheless invades. Tasks left undone during the week must get done on the weekend—yards raked, bills paid, kids shuttled to and fro. The weekend becomes accelerated with different but equally pressing tasks. Unread emails compound on vacation. The taxing catch-up of the first two days back in the office makes you wonder if the vacation was worth it at all. Finally, as you cross the line into retirement, the eternal slowdown quickly imposes a listlessness, a piercing meaninglessness. Within six months, you doubt whether you should have retired in the first place. You decide to start your own small business, assuring yourself that doing so is not reneging on your retirement; it's what your retirement has won you. It's won you the ability to be your own boss of acceleration. Becoming your own boss is another coping illusion of control that promises, but fails, to get acceleration under control. After writing books on the poison of our social acceleration, Rosa realized that slowing down was not the answer.

Another Way of Being: Resonance

To find a real antidote to acceleration, Rosa contends that we'll need a much different form of action, a different way of relating to the world. We'll need a way of being that is not tied to the systems of acceleration. That sounds like a nice fantasy. After all, we're talking about an entirely different form of action, a way of being. And not just for individual people but for society writ large. Societal forms of action can't be created in hermetically sealed laboratories or on the writing desks of German professors. No one, no matter how powerful or perceptive, can create and impose on society a different way of acting, as if pulling a lever. Individuals, let alone societies, don't select kinds of action like they're choosing ice cream flavors. Societies don't make formally reasoned decisions on what constitutes the good life.

Therefore, this different form of action—a way of being that can counter acceleration—needs to be excavated, not created. It must be unearthed from the debris of acceleration, to be found existing alongside acceleration but nevertheless distinct and different in genus. While all our attention has been on time as money, we have always had available another way of being in time. This way of being does not view all our interactions as instruments to be used for growth.

The second half of Rosa's opus of works is dedicated to excavating this other way of being. This other way is indigenous to our human discourse. It has continued to exist even in our modern age because it's bound in address—how we are spoken to and how we address others. This way of being is fundamental to our state as language animals. Pushing this as a metaphor, Rosa contends that this way of being follows the way of sound—experienced in words, music, and tones. He means that in this way of acting and interacting, time is not money (for growth); time is bound in events of encounter, in actions of address, in ways of being heard, seen, and felt. What matters is not growth but distinct voices in mutual but bound vibration, in connections of being addressed and called by something outside of you, apart from you. Rosa calls this form of action "resonance."

Resonance is recognized in a flash of feeling alive, awake, a goosebump moment, a sudden deep awareness and connection. We feel a sense of reverberating with another person or nature, a glimmer of unfettered belonging in the universe. Often tears come. Rosa contends that there are four traits of a resonant experience.

First, something from outside us "calls" to us. Something other than our own self prompts it; we are touched by the world. Perhaps it happens through a stranger's surprising comment that makes us feel seen, the sound of wind in the trees that calls our attention to the intricate beauty of nature, the shared experience with another person of impromptu grief or spontaneous laughter.

Second, a resonant experience requires that we respond, which Rosa calls "self-efficacy." Whether it be that we feel an inner tug of awakening, we notice, we act, we speak, we feel moved to tears, or we reach out and address another in return, resonance elicits a response from us. We answer back.

Third, transformation accompanies resonance. Something shifts. Something changes in the relationship between ourselves and the universe, or between ourselves and one another. We may see the world differently or experience a breakthrough connection with someone or absorb an insight that alters our future actions. When an action of deep belonging, trust, or joy has occurred, the experience stays with us. The dynamic between us and the world is altered.

Finally, a resonant experience is uncontrollable. We can't make it happen.

In his book *Resonance*, Rosa excavates and lays bare this way of being. Like an archaeologist, he brushes away the sand and ash of the fallout of our modern eruption of acceleration to show us the intricate detail and beauty of the underlying geography of resonance.

The Most Important Element: Uncontrollability

This form of action that Rosa calls resonance is fundamentally *uncontrollable*. Uncontrollability reveals that acceleration and resonance are completely different forms of action. They are distinctly different species, like a hippo and a hummingbird. For all the metaphors of hearing, address, and encounter—for all the talk of just being and resting in the now—without the spine of uncontrollability to bolster it, resonance would fall into instrumentalization. Without uncontrollability, resonance would be co-opted and subsumed by the insatiable appetites of acceleration (as we saw when "rest" is saved up and spent on weekends, vacations, and retirement).

After his four-hundred-page tome on resonance, Rosa considered uncontrollability to be such an important point that he felt the need to circle back and center on this one element in his small book *The Uncontrollability of the World*. We'll be using it here to explore the roles of parenting and pastoring, because, we'll contend, both are relational roles intended to welcome shared experiences of resonance but both have largely lost the vital element of uncontrollability. In resonance, the world calls to us, garners a response, and transforms us. But the presence of these three elements, without the fourth—uncontrollability—cannot guard against instrumentalization and the obsessions for growth, as well as the drive for more control. A Nazi rally in the 1930s, for example (which Rosa discusses), can have *most* (all but one) of the elements of resonance. The parade down Unter den Linden is filled with stirring emotion, and the rhetoric of the speeches at the stadium beckons to you (something calls to us). You feel moved to respond in love and willingness to suffer for the fatherland (we respond). The whole experience alters the way you'll be in the world and Deutschland within it (we are transformed). But the one thing the Nazi rally opposes forcefully and completely is the fourth element of resonance: uncontrollability. Uncontrollability is the Nazis' enemy. The rally is a controlled event used as an instrument to help their party take control. This desire for control stretches to the whole world. To them, uncontrollability in all its forms is to be destroyed. Control is the point.

The obsession with control causes acceleration to dominate our imaginations and actions. Even with most of the elements of resonance (except uncontrollability) present, acceleration will continue to rule. Rosa's point is that uncontrollability makes resonance, as a form of action, good. Uncontrollability gives resonance its moral and spiritual (theological) depth. In our parenting and our pastoring, we must embrace uncontrollability.

In Time: Receiving Instead of Using

Inside moments of resonance, such as in a deep conversation with a friend or in the flow of attentiveness to a craft, a painting, or a poem, we are drawn to rest in the now. We are invited to stay and remain with the address, to hear the world speaking to us, calling to us. Such moments are not the weekend, not even a vacation. They are full occasions of being alive in the now, with only this moment to rest inside.

Acceleration, which actively resists rest, tends to view all people as competition. Our actions with and for others are to be used as instruments for gain and growth. We are trying to *use* time, and therefore we shape our relationships to win the resources needed to feel fulfilled or even the resources that will enable us to rest and slow down in time. Yet, when we're pulled into encounters of resonance—being addressed by a friend only for the sake of being together, or encountering the beauty of the mountains that speak to the longing of our soul—we don't *use* time or our relationships in time. Rather, we *receive* time. We see these experiences as gifts. We live inside such moments of address as a form of connection. Their goodness is not in what they win us but in their simple invitation to be—to be together, to hear and speak and connect, to be alive.

Rosa contends that we can find a way of being beyond acceleration in such relationships, inside such actions that are noninstrumental encounters, a way of being where time is not money but full of connections and conversations. Acceleration is a way of seeking to *have* the world. Resonance is a way of *being* in the world.

This longing for resonance prompted us toward the idea of a pilgrimage in the first place. We were seeking to intentionally

16

practice a kind of deliberate attentiveness that allows for the possibility of connection and aliveness with one another, God, and the world. We wanted to find a way to walk the same pace as that of our spirits and souls, to match our feet to our hearts and bodies, and to invite ourselves to be in the world. To receive what we are experiencing.

Attuning to Resonance Through Sabbath

There are two ways of moving in time that are temporarily disconnected from the message and attraction of control. One way of being in time differently, living with an openness to resonance and a willingness to embrace uncontrollability, is offered to us, commanded actually, by God as sabbath. Sabbath is not just slowing down, as we would on a vacation, which only keeps our minds and hearts trapped in the destructive system that dehumanizes and disconnects us. Sabbath is not racing to accumulate the rest we need to perform better and move faster. Sabbath rest is letting go completely, surrendering control, being in the world in an alternate form of action. Practicing sabbath cultivates availability to resonance. Through sabbath we regularly step out of the way of being that defines the goal of life and the value of a human being in terms of producing, controlling, comparing, competing—coming again to the ground of our own being, our own nothingness, in the very being of God. Sabbath is a way of attuning ourselves to the possibility of encounter with God and others. Without intentional, regular rest, we lose sight of our place alongside others in the care of God and we diminish our openness to resonance.

Sabbath rest is not achieved once our work is finished, nor is it earned through time and effort invested. In sabbath rest, time is received as a gift, and thus sabbath invites us to receive our very lives as a gift. In the Jewish practice of *Shabbat*, the moment the sun hits the horizon, we stop. Whether or not to rest is out of our control, and we do not choose when that rest begins; the cycle of the earth around the sun dictates our time, and we surrender to something larger than ourselves.

In sabbath rest, all our human distinctions of worth, value, and order are revealed to be false. We are not gods; we are God's. Any earning or proving, deservingness or unworthiness, all barriers and labels that we use to define or divide ourselves, our very *doing*—everything we're trying to achieve and control by our doing—falls away. We must simply be. Be loved. Beloved, in whom God delights. Alive solely by the breath and word of an uncontrollable God.

In the practice of sabbath, we make ourselves available once more to the music of the universe, the voice of God, the possibility of being addressed by the world. We open ourselves in availability to resonance. In our own family and church, sabbath is something that we have been learning and practicing for going on twenty years. While we still struggle against all the pressures of acceleration, the logic of sabbath has sunk into our beings, and we understand through experience how resting, regularly and intentionally, can open us to encounters of resonance.

EXERCISE: A Twenty-Four-Hour Deep Breath

Preparing for a Sabbath Day

Block out twenty-four hours, evening to evening (e.g., 7 p.m. Saturday to 7 p.m. Sunday). Literally schedule it on your calendar, with nothing allowed to overlap. Think of it as you would a retreat—as though you'll drive three hours to be in a different place. Consider how you might pack for such a trip.

- What would you like to leave behind?
  - » What would feel like a huge relief to put down for twenty-four hours? Would you bring your work laptop or papers to correct? What about your cell phone, social media, or the laundry? Would you want to spend that time away doing

your taxes, preparing for your mother's visit, or fretting about a coworker conflict?

- What, specifically, will you say no to? Write it down: "Tomorrow I will say no to _____" (e.g., screens, shoulds, work).
- What would you like to bring?
  » What would feel like a huge gift to bring into your experience?
  » *Activities:* What activities give you joy or bring you rest? Knitting, napping, drawing, dreaming, reading, relaxing in the bath? What do you need to do in advance to be ready to follow your heart if the moment arises? A good book? Some new yarn? A puzzle? Bring those things to your sabbath retreat. (Be ready to do none of them at all if that's what your soul ends up needing!)
  » *Food:* Would you love a day not to cook? What can you get or do in advance to allow that? Would you love the chance to linger in the kitchen and create a lavish meal? What can you get or do in advance to allow that?
  » *People:* Who in your life will be sharing this experience with you? Children? Spouse? Friends? How can this day be a different kind of day for you all? If you are alone a lot, consider spending part of the day with someone whose company you enjoy. If you're around people a lot, consider finding a pocket of time each person in your house can do something alone, or plan an hour when everyone is quiet together (this can work with kids!). If you will be with a partner or kids, what do you enjoy doing as a family that you don't often make time to do? What can you look forward to together?
- What, particularly, will you say yes to? Write it down: "Tomorrow I will say yes to _____" (e.g., rest, creativity, music).

When Your Ride Leaves

The Jewish sabbath begins exactly at sundown—not by a time on a clock or by someone's to-do list or when everything is finished or when everyone is ready for it. When the sun drops below the horizon, the sabbath has begun. *What's done is done, what is undone remains undone.*

The important thing is that everything gets set down so that space may be opened up within you and between you, so that you can be met by God just as you are. It is a day for *being* instead of *doing*. If you were meeting up with others to board a bus for your sabbath retreat, you would come ready, and when the bus departs you would be on it. So if your start time arrives and you have done no preparing, *do not worry. Get on the bus anyway*—this day will be a blessing to you. It really will!

And if you look ahead to the day and think that, though you intended to take a sabbath day, some super important things came up and you simply do not have time, *all the more reason for you to keep the boundaries of your day set apart. Get on the bus anyway*—this day will be a blessing to you. It *really will.*

Opening and Closing Sabbath Day Prayers

(When the prayers are read as a group, the text in bold font is intended to be read together.)

Beginning Sabbath Time

"Are you tired? Worn out? Weighed down by heaviness? Come to me. Get away with me and you will recover your life. I will show you how to take a real rest. Walk with me and work with me—watch how I do it. Learn the unforced rhythms of grace. I won't lay anything heavy or ill-fitting on you. Keep company with me and you will learn to live freely and lightly." (Matt. 11:28–30, adapted from The Message)

We belong to God, who created us to abide in God's love and
    generosity,
instead of toiling under the rule of an anxious and fearful world.
Be present to us, Lord, in this time set aside.

God, help us let go of _____ (name what you intend to say no
    to today).

We belong to God, who created us for full and joyful life,
and calls us into enduring hope.

Help us be present to you, Lord, in this time set aside.

God, help us embrace _____ *(name what you hope to say yes to today).*

God of creation and rest,
Christ with us in life and death,
Spirit of love, forgiveness, and hope,
we accept your invitation to meet you in sacred time.
Amen.

Ending Sabbath Time

"If God doesn't build the house, the builders only build shacks.
If God doesn't guard the city, the night watchman might as well
    nap.
It's useless to rise early and go to bed late,
and work your worried fingers to the bone.
Don't you know God enjoys giving rest to those God loves?"
(Ps. 127:1–2, adapted from The Message)

We belong to God, who created us to abide in God's love and
    generosity,
instead of toiling under the rule of an anxious and fearful world.
You were present to us, Lord, in this time set aside.

God, thank you especially for _____ *(name what you are
    grateful for, the gifts of this time).*

We belong to God, who created us for full and joyful life,
and calls us into enduring hope.
Help us be present to you, Lord, in our ordinary days.

God, go with us into _____ *(name what you return to: the
    people, circumstances, or tasks you seek to meet with ground-
    edness and trust).*

God of creation and rest,
Christ with us in life and death,
Spirit of love, forgiveness, and hope,
send us out from sacred time
nourished in your rest

and strengthened by your grace.
May we breathe deeper,
surrender more easily,
and carry our loads more lightly.
Amen.

Attuning to Resonance Through Walking (Pilgrimage)

In addition to sabbath, another way we live in time differently, and so make ourselves available to resonance, is by walking. While we modern, believing animals have disconnected most bodily expressions of prayer from our Christian practice, our most basic, simple, ordinary, human, embodied act of putting one foot in front of the other has been woven into our faith story from the beginning.[5] Scripture begins with God walking with Adam and Eve in the garden before they hide themselves from God in mistrust and shame. Throughout the Bible, walking with God, or "walking in the way of the Lord," becomes language for being in right relationship with God, connected and attuned to the divine. Those who are described as "holy" are those who "walk with God" (e.g., Exod. 18:20; Deut. 30:16; 1 Kings 2:3; 2 Kings 22:2; 2 Chron. 34:2; Prov. 2:20; 8:20; Isa. 35:8; Jer. 6:16, just for starters!). Jesus's own ministry began when he walked into the wilderness, and it unfolded through walking as he met people on foot and face-to-face. When Paul wasn't in a boat, his journeys had him walking across the Mediterranean region. The early church simply called Christianity "the Way." Jesus says he *is* the way. Jesus is both the route and the journey, and he walks the human path with and for us at the human pace as the "three-mile-an-hour God."[6] Rather than seeking to transcend our humanity in pursuit of God, we use the practice of prayerfully walking to bring us alongside God-with-us, who walks alongside us in our humanity. Walking slows us to God's pace of love.

Historically, walking pilgrimages—first to Jerusalem and then to other holy sites—have been an integral part of the

Christian faith. To walk in this way is to acknowledge that even more than the destination, it's the *walking toward* that changes you. Pilgrimage is a way of moving the body, will, and spirit in sync into the unknown. With each step a pilgrim confesses that they actually have no control and therefore they have no other hope than the uncontrollable God of the uncontrollable cross. The ancient pilgrim was advised to make a last will and testament before departing, to act as though they were walking to their death. How could they do anything but understand that the pilgrimage is a direct way of preparing to die? After all, there *was* a good chance the pilgrim would never return; the journey was often dangerous. But because it was perilously uncontrollable, there was also a good chance the pilgrim would meet God in the wild uncontrollability of the path.

A pilgrimage is a way to practice orienting ourselves toward resonance. It strips away what distracts us from the basic fact of our being alive, here in this world, held by God, so that we might be in a better position to notice and receive resonance when it occurs. When we simply walk—looking, listening, feeling the ground beneath us and our breath in our lungs—we become present, receiving time instead of consuming it. By simply moving forward in the most basic human way, putting one foot in front of the other, we are making ourselves available to be met on the way by Christ, who is the Way.

Defying Acceleration Logic: A Pilgrimage Is Not a Workout

Just as acceleration hijacks rest, attempting to optimize weekends, vacations, and retirement, so also acceleration tempts us to consider a walking pilgrimage to be no different from a workout. A pilgrimage, however, is something much different. A workout centers the self as the self seeks to overcome its limits through its own performance. But something is askew if a pilgrimage is treated as a form of optimization, because it is a journey into uncontrollability.

In a satisfying workout, a successful 10K, or even a marathon, the perception is that the self controls its will and body and ultimately can overcome all limits. The workout culture that budded in the 1980s, curated by companies such as Nike, contends that if we just sweat and optimize, we can do anything—a powerful message in a late-capitalist age. Consider that every big corporation and hotel chain that caters to executives has a gym. In our age, the workout reinforces the illusion that we can control and master the uncontrollable. The most effective way to get control of our lives, we're told, is by hopping on a Peloton, getting a personal trainer, or buying a new pair of running shoes and a smartwatch. The workout burns calories, but it also trains and readies our spirits for control. The health benefits are often linked with, even coated onto, the self's ability to win control. Control of your cholesterol and abs is just the beginning! You can extend yourself beyond your limits, control your life and your future! The whole wellness movement presents itself as a way to take control of what is ultimately uncontrollable.

But whereas a workout builds up the self so it can move beyond, even deny, death (and therefore supposedly control it), a pilgrimage enters directly into death to drop the pilgrim into uncontrollability. The point of the pilgrimage is not to get fit or accomplish something grand. The purpose is to let go of all illusions that you have any ability to control any part of the world whatsoever.

A walking pilgrimage is the *exact opposite* of the modern workout. Through the simple act of putting one foot in front of the other, over and over again, a pilgrimage reflects the journey of the whole of our lives—a journey we moderns, and modernity itself, seek both to deny and to overcome. At both its best and its worst, life is uncontrollable. Here in the unknown and uncontrollable—the pilgrim wagers—we find life because we find the God who remains always uncontrollable as true God. Rather than pursuing self-optimization, we enter and embrace uncontrollability in order to recognize, like the sad pilgrims discovered on the road to Emmaus (Luke 24), that the living God is indeed with us, on the trail of life alongside us, most directly when life is at its most uncontrollable.

The two of us are uncomfortable recognizing the many ways our parenting has fit inside the acceleration logic of a workout more than the three-mile-an-hour logic of a pilgrimage. Church leadership can easily be the same way. In both cases, we often fail to see our role as helping people seek the uncontrollable God in the unexpected flourishing and bewildering desolation through which we all journey. Instead of preparing our kids to receive this life and all that it holds with responsive openness, we want to give them more resources for success, push them to be the best they can be, and assist them in the unspoken eschatological attempt to deny death. In the church we may use words like "growing," "building," "enlivening," and "revitalizing," but what we're generally after is more control to achieve more results to fend off what feels like the inevitable death of the church if not for our own herculean efforts. And so, we mostly do not seek God in the wild and uncontrollable places.

Leading Our Children and Congregations Toward Uncontrollability

Without realizing this would happen when we started out, our sixty-three-(plus-)mile pilgrimage on St. Cuthbert's Way through Scotland and England would come to reveal its purpose to us in shocking awareness and poignant consciousness. This was to be a journey of letting go of our children. We would feel ourselves setting them on the path of uncontrollability, a path we could not—and should not—control. Each step would remind us that they have their own lifetime to live, their own death to prepare for. We can't hide them from this. We can no longer hide it from ourselves.

Journeying alongside our kids and each other through a story of the church older than we could comprehend, we would come to find that here too we're being welcomed into uncontrollability. Perhaps the invitation of this pilgrimage would prompt us to release not just the temptation to control the road for our kids but also the tendency to infantilize the church. Maybe the whole point of both our pastoring and our parenting is to let go of control.

If we wish for our parenting or our leading in the church to be alive, forming us and those we love—addressing, connecting, avoiding the pitfalls of instrumentalization—then it is necessary to do what is unnatural inside modernity: find ways to let go of control and enter the pilgrim's way of uncontrollability. If we want to be open to resonance, to practice a way of being in which we hear the world speaking and are moved and transformed, we must embrace and even seek uncontrollability. In our families and congregations, whether as parents, pastors, church staff, elders, or volunteers, leadership in the way of God must be a journey into uncontrollability.

2

The Thrill of Uncontrollability

It's All in the Timing

The idea took hold sometime in 2020. But that year is such a fog that we can't remember exactly when or how. It started with Kara. A year or two before, she'd begun dreaming of walking a pilgrimage as a spiritual practice of listening to God and being open to the world. She researched a few cool-weather, doable walks, bought a couple of books, and let the idea simmer.

Then in 2020, Andy suggested, "What if we all did a pilgrimage together?" Remember, people were saying all sorts of crazy things in 2020—"I'm going to bake with sourdough" or "I want to learn to knit." (Kara did the sourdough thing, forcing the family to eat sourdough everything. The rest of us now hate sourdough because of it.) Kara knew people who had walked parts of the Camino de Santiago. When our kids were young, we'd driven from Paris to Mont-Saint-Michel in northern France. On that trip we imagined being medieval pilgrims and walking there. We envisioned what it would have been like to see the majestic monastery rising out of the sea like a huge horn. Approaching barefoot on the damp mudflats of a receding sea (similar to Lindisfarne), we contemplated what it would have been like hundreds of years ago to view it as a faint speck on the horizon after a long journey, to draw closer and closer and eventually to stand below it as it towered over us, knowing we'd finally arrived.

We also just like to walk, which began when we were students in Princeton and money was tight. For entertainment, we'd go into New York City and just walk. Walking has been our thing ever since. When we visit a city, we walk it. Some of our best (and worst!) times as a family have been walking cities like Paris, London, Berlin, Tokyo, and Sydney. Walking cities, we've had some of our family's deepest philosophical conversations, greatest raucous belly laughs, and most outrageous, furious arguments.

It made sense for Kara's dream of a walking pilgrimage to expand to include the whole family. We circled August 2020 as the target. Andy booked tickets. It was supposed to be a big year of travel for us. Our son Owen was set to go on a mission trip to Mexico, and we were going to take Andy's mom to Amsterdam, Berlin, and Prague. In the early weeks of 2020, everything was falling into place. Plans were coming together. Owen's freshman year of high school was going very well, and our daughter Maisy had comfortably adjusted to middle school. When the first weeks of the pandemic arrived in March, we were concerned but certain, like everyone, that by early summer it would all be behind us.

Then, just hours before Owen was to leave, with his bags packed and loaded into the car, his mission trip was canceled. The dominos fell from there. One by one, everything dropped from the calendar. Maisy now needed to adjust to online middle school, and all of Owen's high school momentum came to a garish thud. And a scary one at that. He spent the next eighteen months alone in his room, nearly twenty-three hours a day. For him, the pandemic started as an introvert's dream but got darker and darker, turning into a nightmare as time passed. His grades plummeted and the isolation hardened. There were days we figured Owen didn't move more than two hundred steps. None of our cajoling worked, nothing extracted him from his room. Finally, in winter 2022, the prodding turned into intervention. All we could think to do was the most basic human act: walk. We had tried so much else and were at a loss. We figured we walked the dog because she needed us to take her—she could not go on her own. Maybe Owen was the same way. So we decided to start walking him. Each afternoon when it was time to walk the dog, we walked our son as well. It made a difference. It possibly opened the door to much more, but that's his story to tell.

We had rescheduled the pilgrimage for summer 2021, and just in time for summer the European Union reopened to visitors. But the UK and particularly Scotland hadn't opened—not without mandatory quarantines. We thought about shifting things and walking part of the Camino de Santiago or even a pilgrim's path into Rome. But by now St. Cuthbert's Way and the Borderlands had gotten hold of our imaginations. It was Cuthbert or bust. We can't say why; we just felt connected to that plan. We needed to wait. Finally, in late summer 2022—two years late—we were ready to fly to Edinburgh and begin our walk. Maisy was now a sophomore and Owen moving into his senior year. They'd both become young adults during the two-year pause. Owen had gone from not moving more than a few hundred steps to walking on his own seven to ten miles a day. We were ready, and it seemed in God's providence that the timing was just right.

Who Is St. Cuthbert?

Cuthbert is an interesting person, to say the least. Since his death in 687, he's become *the* patron saint of the North, particularly of Northumberland and Cumbria, in England. Even in the secular society of the UK, where self-reported Christians have fallen to under 50 percent of the population[1] (where the Newcastle football club finds more passionate and loyal support than the church does), Cuthbert remains venerated. He is esteemed as much as Newcastle's top striker. Perhaps Cuthbert was destined to be the great saint of the North even from birth. Cuthbert was born in 634, the same year that the great Aiden laid the first stones of the abbey on Lindisfarne—the place where Cuthbert's body would be interred after his last day. His body lay there untouched by the decay of death, by the will of God radiating a holiness that healed. For over 1,400 years Lindisfarne and Cuthbert have been inseparably intertwined. It's quite amazing that they were born together, the same year, linked even before they were linked.

Yet, even with all the respect and lore that surrounds Cuthbert—or maybe because of it—he's a hard nut to crack. Unlike with our other theological and mystical heroes, nothing directly from Cuthbert's own head or hand has survived. There are no sermons like Meister Eckhart's, no meditations like Teresa of Ávila's, no biblical exegesis like Gregory of Nyssa's, and no treatises like Ambrose's. Nothing comes to us directly from Cuthbert's own hand and therefore his own mind. There seems to be no way into Cuthbert's head, no way to unpack, deconstruct, and rearrange his ideas, letting them speak into a different time. Unlike the others we've just named, Cuthbert's inner life is silent.

Even his actions are shrouded in mystery and myth. What we have from Cuthbert are stories of his lore that have shaped the North. But for the stories to do their shaping they needed to be written down. This task of recording Cuthbert's great works fell to a monk who never directly knew him. The monk nevertheless felt called to record what was reported about Cuthbert by those who did know him. This young monk, Bede, was quite talented with the pen. He put on the page the miraculous tales of Cuthbert, making Bede posthumous Robin to Cuthbert's Batman. Their final resting places are just meters apart from each other in the Durham Cathedral.

The Man of the North

Cuthbert, from head to toe and everything in between, was a man of the North. The damp, cold chills of that part of the world ran through his blood, mingling with his cells. That same gray sky continues to animate his lore. Cuthbert, since his death, has been as much a staple of the North as the sea and salt air.

Maybe we were drawn to Cuthbert because we too are people of the North, though a much different kind of North on a much different continent. There is no salt in our frigid northern air. But we are nevertheless northerners. Minnesotans. The North's cold and snow, its trees and lakes, window scrapers and jumper cables, are part of us. While a handful of our most formative young adult years happened elsewhere, nearly the whole of both our lives has been lived in the North.

Our North contains humid, mosquito-filled evenings when neighbors congregate outdoors in all manner of convivial scenes under a sky that stays lit until after 10 p.m. Bright emerald trees dipped like paintbrushes into reds and oranges that eventually flame out and drop to the scruffy ground, fading the world to bare. The deadening and hardening of the frozen earth, our breath visible in the icy wind that numbs our cheeks while the world pulls on its heavy, white blanket to hide for long months beneath the cobalt sky's brilliant arctic sun. Then, just when it feels like the deep freeze of winter will last forever, the ecstatic welcome of the muddy spring melt that drags its feet, finally exploding the world into bloom.

The coarse beauty of the North has done its work in the background and interior of our lives to shape our spirits, as

31

it did with Cuthbert. In retrospect, it's little surprise that the saint of the North would connect with our imaginations, even though there is nothing from Cuthbert's own heart or thoughts for us to read. His silence may be what makes him a true man of the North. Just like with our grandfathers, it's permitted, even in the posterity of a millennium and a half, for his actions to speak more than his words.

The Man of Solitude

In Cuthbert's day, solitude and the desert were intertwined like PB&J. It had been this way since Anthony of Alexandria (Anthony the Great) walked into the Egyptian desert in 270, giving himself over to grueling seclusion for the sake of praying for the world and communing with the Holy Spirit. Anthony's demand for isolation in the desert created a problem that put the poor monks of northern England, Scotland, and Ireland at a great disadvantage. There were no deserts in the British Isles. There were, however, seas. If the desert was an expanse of harsh loneliness, in which the monk would be forced to trust only God, so too was the sea. The sea was its own kind of desert seclusion.

Cuthbert craved solitude. After serving as bishop (over and against his deepest desire), Cuthbert retreated to Lindisfarne. He wanted to forget the many political battles that had taken their toll. But even the abbey on Lindisfarne was too much for Cuthbert. He longed for the extreme solitude of the great mystics. Lindisfarne, though itself an island, was not enough of a desert—not like Anthony's Egyptian desert. There were too many other monks, and it wasn't far enough into the sea. And so, like Yoda on the Dagobah system, Cuthbert prepared himself for a more rugged and wet solitude. Cuthbert departed the abbey to go to a much smaller island, several miles into the sea from Lindisfarne (you can just barely see the island of Farne from the hill next to the abbey). There Cuthbert would be truly alone to battle his will and empty his soul in solitary privacy.

Arriving, it was all more Yoda than even Yoda. Cuthbert had to first sweep the island of evil forces, casting shadowy demons into the sea. Then, with the help of charitable animals, he found food and built a place to sleep and pray. It was in this complete isolation that Cuthbert stayed and eventually died. This was just as Cuthbert wanted it. He wanted to die in prayer and total seclusion, like the great mystics before him.

During the height of the pandemic, we became infatuated with the History channel show *Alone*, where people brave the harsh elements armed with only a camera and their wits to compete to last the longest while living completely alone in the wild. The gripping interplay between control and the uncontrollable drew us in. Against the backdrop of the whole world feeling uncontrollable, it was strangely cathartic watching people navigate the uncontrollable wilderness with pinpoint focus on just food, shelter, heat, and water, while enduring the real test: solitude. Reading of Cuthbert's quest for seclusion alongside these nightly glimpses into a modern struggle to endure solitude brought Cuthbert's story to life.

The Man of (Dead Guy) Miracles

Discovering that Cuthbert had passed, the monks of the abbey of Lindisfarne retrieved his body, burying it near the abbey next to the other bishops and priors. Yet, though Cuthbert was dead, he kept doing stuff. The great king of Wessex, Alfred, had a dream of Cuthbert. In the dream, Cuthbert compelled Alfred to stand up to the invading Danes. Others, too, even before Alfred's dream, had found healing and restoration when praying near Cuthbert's remains. A young boy had a demon cast out of him when he drank the water in which the monks bathed Cuthbert's dead body. (Very gross but liberating for the boy!)

After eleven years dead, per custom, Cuthbert's body was exhumed. The idea was to gather the bones so they might be stored in a sarcophagus in the little church. But to the monks' shock, Cuthbert's body remained completely intact, without decomposition. The monks were astonished but perhaps not surprised. The miracles were proof of what had become obvious. There was so much holiness running through the weathered body of the old northern cleric that death itself could not break down his remains.

The holiness of Jesus Christ is bound inseparably to Jesus's own body overcoming death. As the resurrection testifies, death has no ability to hold down Jesus. For Cuthbert to be conformed to Jesus, to have his Spirit running through his own body, would mean that the signs of death could not corrupt his body. Death could take Cuthbert's life, but death could not sully his body. (Not for the first eleven years, at least.)

Cuthbert was just a creature, like the otters and sea lions that attended to him when he prayed (more on this later). All creatures die. Jesus's resurrection into eternal life testifies that while Christ was indeed a creature, and therefore bound in a body, he was also the creator. For only one begotten but *not* made can live bodily, though he has died bodily. Cuthbert died. He was a creature, begotten and made. As such, death holds him down on this side of the eschaton. But Cuthbert died so bathed in the holiness of the Spirit of Christ that though he was dead, his remains continued to pulse with the holiness of Jesus's own life. The monks contended that Cuthbert's corpse was so imbued with holiness that his remains themselves were used by God to perform miraculous healings.

Bede never met Cuthbert. Bede was too young to know him. But Bede knew and researched the stories, and he himself experienced the miracles of Cuthbert's corpse.

As we read Cuthbert's lore, the mystery of the miracles drew us in. Living through a pandemic will do that to you;

doomscrolling will make you either despair or long for a miracle, or perhaps both simultaneously. About five months into the pandemic, Andy stopped sleeping.

Each night my mind started racing around 3 a.m., resisting all soothing encouragement to return to sleep. Each morning brought a desperate longing for a miracle, meeting me bright and early with anxious dread. I felt like I was being abducted by an invisible force. I was frantic to escape. This desperation was paired with a sullen, sharp sting of what had been lost. What other plans were being pulled toward the precipice, soon to be pushed over the cliff to crash on rocks of canceled? *What other lost dreams would meet me each morning? I ate breakfast and read the news before 4 a.m., longing desperately for a story to appear of some breakthrough or new turn with the virus, or maybe just some new technology to free us. Every bowl of early morning cereal was equal parts Wheaties, milk, and foreboding, and almost always more bad news.*

Yet, each morning, Andy again hoped for a miracle.

The North of Cuthbert and Bede radiated with the miraculous, something we longed for in our own cold North of the pandemic. As the snow fell on the icy winter of the end of 2020 and the beginning of 2021, we watched on TV the corpses piling up across the world. Places like New York City were forced to create temporary morgues, parking lots filled with freezer trucks. There were too many bodies, too many corpses overtaken by the virus. We watched and yearned for a miracle as body bags were stacked and nurses pleaded for help in worn-out PPE. The world needed a miracle.

The Thrill of Uncontrollability: Rosa Starts with Snow

Rosa begins *The Uncontrollability of the World* with the invitation to recall when you saw falling snow for the first time. When did you first watch the white flakes swirl and drop from the sky from as far up as you could see? Remember how you allowed them to land on your face? Even opening your mouth to welcome the cold flakes to melt on your warm tongue? There's a stillness, a vastness, a receptivity demanded by falling snow. As children we wanted to be inside the snowfall, to take it all in, so much so that we couldn't resist tasting a bit of the snow. (In the North we are taught, even before we can tie our own shoes, to eat only freshly fallen snow and *especially* never yellow snow.)

As children of the North, we knew that when the temperature dropped and the grass went brown, it would soon snow. But the first snowfall was always magical anyway (and still is). The first snow, with its meager inch or two, brings a jolt of wonder. What had been so familiar—the grass, the trees, the driveway—is now different. The snow brings us into a new world. What was—the wide streets, open sidewalks, shrubs, flowers, mown grass, green leaves—is gone, not to be seen again for months. We are suddenly now citizens of another place. When the Pevensie children go through the wardrobe in C. S. Lewis's Narnia books, they enter a landscape swathed in snow. Snow is a sure sign of being in a different world. The blanket of snow changes everything, remaking the world as we once knew it. Even darkness is different after snow covers the ground and roofs. Nights are colder but brighter. The moon's light reflects off the white wonderland, making the snow itself glimmer with the light of the twinkling stars. Sleeping in summer means closing our shades to the bright morning light that wakes us early. The winter reverses things so that the mornings are dark but the nights are bright. We find ourselves closing the shades to the winter landscape that reflects the light of the moon.

Rosa begins his book with snow because there is no controlling the snow. There is no way to force this new world to come. The snow cannot be cajoled to fall. It would certainly be convenient if it could; it would sure help with planning.

Meteorologists make projections and farmers have informed guesses, but no one knows for sure when the first snow is coming. Which is what makes it so exciting. There is little more magical than the uncontrollable snow falling on Christmas Eve. In Minnesota (until recently) we've rarely worried about whether it will be a white Christmas. Historically, by Christmas we've had a half dozen or more significant snowfalls, with a good seven or eight inches on the ground before the end of Advent. But for those not so north, or those whose north is closer to the sea, the hope and anticipation of a potentially white Christmas is significant. It is for Rosa. He writes, "So many people—not only children—long for [the snow], especially around the holidays. Meteorologists are assailed and beseeched for weekends beforehand. Will it be a white Christmas this year? What are the chances?"[2]

The uncontrollability of the snow is what makes it powerfully stirring. Yet its ability to move us is exactly what tempts us to seek to control it. Its thrill makes us want to possess what cannot be controlled. Whether we're a child in awe or a corporation needing profits, we try to possess the snow. The child who loves the snow, stirred by its wonder, wants to save it. They put a snowball (or a whole snowman!) in the freezer. Who hasn't tried this? But saved snow spoils, like the Israelites' manna. Or more accurately, snow hardens into lifeless ice. Snow bound in captivity loses its life.

Instead of putting snow in captivity, we just mechanically produce as much of it as we want! Ski resorts invest big money in snow-making machines. They can't depend on profits if their customers can't depend on snow. With machines making artificial snow, resorts can guarantee skiers and snowboarders snow until Memorial Day in some places. While every skier and snowboarder will attest that fresh, natural snow is best, the top runs must nevertheless invest in such machines. Real snow is just uncontrollable, and uncontrollability is bad for growth-based businesses. Investors prefer (throw their money at) businesses that can control as high a percentage of the variable of uncontrollability as possible. The higher the percentage, the more assured the investor is on their capital gains.

Make Us Be Moved

We are pulled between two poles. What makes us modern is that we're always being yanked, sometimes violently and other times more subtly, between these two poles: control and uncontrollability. But this is not like a tug-of-war, in which two sides stand in direct opposition, jerking and dragging each other. There is no either/or here. It's not as though you can completely choose "team control" or "team uncontrollability."

We become obsessed with control because of the alluring invitation of certain forms of uncontrollability. We are so moved by the uncontrollability of the snow that our modern inclination, and therefore imagination, turns to how we might control it.

We love our children so much, wanting the best for them, because we've been so moved by their uncontrollable presence. Thus we seek to control them, fearing we might lose them. We become sure that *we* cannot be happy if *they* aren't happy. We control their lives so that they (and we) might have more (un)controllable happiness.

Similarly, we have encountered the uncontrollable presence of God in our congregations. We've experienced the uncontrollable moments of being in community or having the Scriptures speak to us. As with our children, we're tempted into trying to control such uncontrollable encounters. We come to see the church not as a space where together people await the uncontrollable God but as a place of controlled programs that promise benefit returns on investment.

We are deeply moved by the uncontrollable, leading us moderns to tragically become anxious about how we might control what is fundamentally uncontrollable. Not so much because we love control (though there is some of that) or even because we fear the uncontrollable, which we certainly do. We also try to wield control because we've been awakened to the magic of snow: We long for the uncontrollable.

This tension between control and uncontrollability is the womb of modern genius and modern anguish, modern charity and modern evil. Our technologies and institutional structures, for good and bad, are mobilized by the desire to control the uncontrollable.

This is the curse of being modern: We fly close to the sun, thinking we can control its rays and heat. To be modern is not to be a rational machine-like operator without emotion, like Spock from *Star Trek*. It is not to be an unmoved force. For all its attention on rationality and the empirical, modernity overflows with emotion. Modernity is soaked with a desire to be moved. We moderns are so moved by the beauty and horror of the uncontrollable that we go to the greatest of lengths (even polluting our own planet) to make the world—the snow, our children, our spirituality—controllable. We cannot accept that some things (some of the most important things) are uncontrollable. Instead of accepting uncontrollability with communal rituals and narratives of God's act in the world, we either seek to protect ourselves from uncontrollability or attempt to actually *possess* uncontrollability for ourselves. Moved by the uncontrollable, our response is not to accept the uncontrollable and be shaped by it but instead to forget we are creatures at all. We believe we can shape the uncontrollable for our own use.

This pursuit would be so clearly absurd if we moderns weren't so good at it. We've been so successful at producing control out of the uncontrollable that it's ironically made us anxious and depressed (exhausted). The amount of energy necessary to corral the uncontrollable behind fences of control will do that. If not for our shiny snow machines, clever parenting methods, and high-output megachurches, we'd more easily see that this is all a tragic folly. (TV shows like *The Walking Dead* or *The Last of Us* and the book of Ecclesiastes unpack just this folly.)

Even so, we moderns feel something is lost. There is something we're missing—hence the anxiety and depression. We've come to assume that the only medicine to treat the unease of not being able to completely corral the uncontrollable is more control. We are addicts that way—the drug that makes us sick is the only thing that brings relief.

The two of us know this feeling all too well. As we readied things for our pilgrimage—having mentally and emotionally prepared for years and logistically planned for months, getting all the details down pat—we found ourselves in a helpless and tenuous situation. Our own drive to control the uncontrollable became uncomfortably tangible as the time for our departure approached.

Eleven days before departure, Maisy tested positive for COVID.

Pre-Pilgrimage Uncontrollability: Day Minus-Three

We are scheduled to leave in three days. Maisy has been quarantined in the basement for a week. Every day we wake up and study ourselves for symptoms, wondering if today will be the day another one of us gets sick and our whole trip gets canceled. So far, we're all fine—poor Maisy herself has been fine for days, but out of an abundance of caution (and to exert what little control we have), we've kept her closed up in the basement, day after boring, lonely day, delivering her meals on a tray and conveying our affection over FaceTime. Owen has plans to go out tonight, and he works tomorrow. That makes us nervous and worried. Everything makes us nervous and worried. We're really trying not to be nervous and worried.

In the middle of the night after Maisy first tests positive, Kara wakes with a start and the knowledge floods in. Fear and anxiety rise up like a monster. In the half sleep of the deep night another thought breaks through: *The goal of this pilgrimage is to surrender to God, to be led by God, to be open to God. God always moves in impossibility. Why wouldn't this pilgrimage also begin in impossibility? Why wouldn't we need to start trusting God before we even depart?* Consciously surrendering, she feels the anxiety flow out as quickly and surely as it rushed in, and miraculously she falls back to sleep.

The week has been filled with this ebb and flow, anxiety back to trust, or if not trust at least living in the moment. But somehow that also makes the week feel luxuriously long. Each day when we wake up, our minds jump forward and then contract back, "Oh wait! It's only Thursday!" Each day buys us more time to either develop symptoms or feel closer to being out of the woods.

Now it's softly raining, drumming on the roof and dripping from the eaves, and the breeze wafting through the screen smells like damp earth. We've just finished booking all the dinner plans for all the stops on the journey. The morning, midday, and evening prayer cards are printed and laminated. The dogsitter is fully prepped. We're eating down the veggies in the fridge. We keep inching forward, testing each step, and then planting a foot. God willing, we will leave in three days.

A Prayer for Surrender

O Lord,
Give me courage to face the nothingness in me
and in the world.
Help me to surrender my striving for somethingness
and all the tools I use to measure my worth.

Take away the things that are killing me,
knock over the things that are propping me up,
remove all obstacles preventing me
from receiving your love and welcoming your grace.

Where I am lost, Lord, find me.
Shake me out of unrest
that I may return to rest.
Free me from estrangement
that I may be connected once again.
Bring me back to the core of my being,
the deepest part of me that recognizes you
and knows what it is to be me—beloved, belonging, and free.

Summon me back
into the hope that does not disappoint.
Immerse me in your love.
Return me to you, the Source of my life,
that I may be fully alive.
Let me be fully alive.
Amen.

Source: Kara K. Root, *Receiving This Life* (Fortress, 2023), 117.

3

Get Aggressive, Get, Get Aggressive

Beginning

We've landed in Edinburgh! It's official: The pilgrimage is on. As far as we know, there are no connections between Cuthbert and Edinburgh. Edinburgh plays a weighty part in the history of modern philosophy and post-Reformation theology but no real part in the life of Cuthbert. The story of Cuthbert and his pilgrim's way starts south of Edinburgh in Melrose, a beautiful little Scottish village next to the Tweed River.

It's early morning when we exit the airport and take a train into the city. The Fringe Festival has engulfed Edinburgh. The energy is lively and light. Street performers and musicians fill the air around their staked-out corners with banter and music, whether peppy or plaintive. We hang around a craft market for a few minutes and, already exhausted and famished, eat our breakfast outside the doors of a pub near the train station.

Our flight left home at 3 p.m. with a layover in Amsterdam, so we've had little to no sleep, except for Ambien Andy. The breakfast energizes us. We stroll around Edinburgh for a couple hours, taking in the architecture and soaking up the vitality, just dipping our toes into this beautiful city. It's sunny and pleasant. Maisy gets acquainted with her new camera as we stretch our legs in a small park and put our feet in the grass to combat jet lag.

In the afternoon we board a train to Tweedbank and arrive in a small, provincial station. There's almost nobody around. Our kids are not happy that we've decided—with all our luggage—to walk the two miles to Melrose. We figure it's a good idea to keep our legs moving, letting the blood circulate after sitting on a plane for ten hours. Our kids figure we're nuts, too cheap to pay for a cab—which isn't completely wrong.

Pulling up directions on a phone, we drag our bags along a pebble-strewn dirt path aside the Tweed River and finally enter the town of Melrose. It is a beautiful little village. We find our quaint inn, where we eagerly shower and change clothes. The old abbey ruins stand majestically against the sky just a few blocks from our hotel. We decide it's best to visit them in the morning; we're too tired now. That turns out to be a mistake.

We eat an early dinner at a small nearby pub with an outdoor deck. We are not super hungry for food, but we're ravenous for sleep, and we know from experience that it's important to eat before we succumb to the first night's travel coma, lest we wake in the middle of the night too hungry to keep sleeping. A few other groups of people are eating on the deck around us, laughing and talking. Two workers are replacing the roof tiles next to the seating area, one on the roof and one standing on a ladder. The party at the table next to us heckles them good-naturedly. The hecklers' dog, DJ, jumps off their bench and strolls confidently over to greet us. He climbs onto our table and, without hesitating, settles happily in Andy's lap, turning to lick Maisy's face. His owners admonish him playfully in rich Scottish brogue, just as they had the roofers. He briefly acknowledges then mostly ignores them, and Maisy is delighted.

We're all a bit out-of-body with fatigue and trying to hang on to consciousness in these last hours of the day. Owen didn't even make it to the pub with us; he's already out cold. We'll place a snack on his bedside table for his inevitable midnight munchies.

Returning to our rooms, we fall into bed and are asleep almost immediately.

Cuthbert's First Call: Through a Child

What led Cuthbert to arrive at the abbey in Melrose can be traced to two events. The first comes from childhood. Aside from his birth in 634, there is not much we know about Cuthbert's childhood. The assumption is that he was a strong, athletic boy from a family of means. This presumption is based on him being a soldier of some success as a young man, perhaps even a knight, fighting in northern conflicts. Other saints and mystics of the later medieval period had similar backgrounds, particularly in the Germanic nations. Eckhart's father, it's believed, was a knight, and the mysterious Frankfurter of the *Theologia Germanica* tells his readers that he is a knight. But ultimately, what assures us that Cuthbert came from a family of means is that when he arrived at the abbey in Melrose, giving himself over to the monastic life, Cuthbert appeared on a horse. A white horse actually, if we can trust the depiction of the scene on the plates (plate seven) that accompany Bede's *Life of Cuthbert*. Arriving on a white horse—on any horse at all—would be like pulling up today at the front of a monastery in a souped-up, bright yellow Ferrari. Such a statement couldn't be ignored: This young man is turning from significant standing to enter the monastic life. He comes from somewhere. His family's got dough. They are important.

The story goes that the well-bred Cuthbert was wrestling with the other boys of his village, goofing around with them, tussling and pushing. Just then a small child became disturbed with Cuthbert's nonsense. The small boy shouted, "Cuthbert, when will you put away such foolish behavior?"

Cuthbert is halted in his steps. He looks inquisitively into the little boy's eyes (not something that someone of Cuthbert's

Cuthbert arriving at the abbey in Melrose on a white horse

stature would likely do to someone beneath him). But Cuthbert has already been violating the rules of propriety—he's been rolling in the northern mud with peasant boys. The eye-to-eye look signals that Cuthbert is open to hearing a word from the boy's mouth as though from God.

The boy throws himself to the ground, crying. Cuthbert comforts him. Again, an act beneath a noble (but fitting for a great pastor). As Cuthbert embraces the boy, from his little mouth the child repeats his claim that Cuthbert is acting a fool. The boy through tears asks young Cuthbert how he, chosen by God to be God's servant and bishop (major prophecy here!), could be playing such foolish games when he was called in wisdom to lead the North into righteousness?

This story shares a fascinating correlation with a child's prophesy in Augustine's life. Both Cuthbert and Augustine live wildly in their youth. For both young men their calling comes inside this foolishness. Augustine provides more detail, but he too is acting a fool, like Cuthbert. Augustine steals pears for no other reason than to commit vandalism, and he loves to party with his friends, enjoying women and drink. As a young man Augustine visits Milan to see the master teacher Ambrose at work. As he is sitting one day in a garden, he hears the voice of a small child say to him, "Pick up and read." Beside him is the book of Romans. Augustine picks up the book and begins reading. The words inside stir him and call him into the Christian faith and eventually as bishop of Hippo. For both Cuthbert and Augustine the story of their calling is fused with the proclamation of a child who awakens them from their foolishness.

Why would it not be a child? Why wouldn't the calling of two of the church's greatest saints be bound to the words of a small child? The heart of the Christian confession is that the Christ child is the very true God of true God, born to and cared for by a mother. God comes into the world as a child in Nazareth, never not the child of Mary, never free of her care and parenting. God comes into the world uncontrollably (entering impossibly into the virgin womb of a teenager, and Mary confesses in her Magnificat that this is all so uncontrollably frightening and fantastic). Even so, this uncontrollable God comes into the world to be held as a child, parented inside the uncontrollable confession that this Jesus, son of Mary, is true God of true God, begotten (and therefore enterally a child as Son to Father) but not made. Therefore, though a child, Jesus is true God, in all ways true God.

Christianity is the faith of children. Jesus makes that clear in Matthew 19. The Christian confession asserts that the universe is made and held (and all its ills overcome) by *the* child. When we center children in the life of the congregation, we open ourselves to the presence of God in concrete and tangible ways. Children are not merely recipients of a congregation's ministry; they are ministers themselves. When we parent our children with listening and not just telling, receiving and not just instructing, we open ourselves to the wisdom of God, which often meets us in the voice of our children. We are accompanied by those who have not yet fully absorbed the messages of the need for control and thus are more open to resonance.

Church Practices Centering Children

There are many ways for congregations to move from ministry *to* children to embracing the ministry *of* children. Years ago, we shifted our "children's message" in worship from the pastor speaking to the children to the children teaching the congregation. In Sunday school beforehand, the children would prepare a short lesson about the day's Scripture text to present to the congregation through an art project, puppet show, Q&A, or drama. Children create and lead the prayer we use after the offering, draw sermon illustrations during worship that are shared at the end, and often serve as greeters and ushers in worship. Intergenerational and formational experiences can offer activities like "blessing scavenger hunts," joint art-making, or baking together that allow for conversation, storytelling, and interaction across supposed age barriers. Matching adults to kids as prayer partners or homebound members to families with young children for occasional visits, turning VBS into an all-ages program, and helping children contribute in "adult" ways, such as reading Scripture in worship, all recognize the ministry of children among us. These activities open us to the mystery of a God who joins us in the Christ child.

It shouldn't surprise us that the calling of two of the church's greatest pastors comes from children—and mysteriously so. The Christ child is the mystery of the fullness of God. In a similar mystery, a small child tells Cuthbert to stop messing around and recognize that he is called to be a bishop. Both

Cuthbert and Augustine are reluctant but important bishops whose calling to the office, to the faith of the Christ child himself, comes through the voice of a little one.

Pilgrimage, Day 1: Melrose to St. Boswells

The sun is streaming in the windows of the dining room in Melrose and breakfast is lovely. Maisy valiantly tries coffee again but is still not a fan. As we check out of our hotel, Kara strikes up a conversation with two women outfitted for serious walking. They're holding metal poles and wearing the proper protective hats, wicking garments, and sturdy shoes. It's our first encounter with fellow pilgrims, and they're experienced trail walkers—intending to cover our first two days' walk in one. They're impressed we are traveling with our children and seem slightly relieved not to be held back, as we inevitably will be. But we also trust that journeying with our children will open us to a kind of wisdom, attentiveness, and receptivity that we would miss if we were doing this trek all rushed and adulty. Children may slow us down, but they also carry less baggage than we do. Our journey will undoubtedly be vastly different from these women's. We wish them well and never see them again.

Cuthbert's Second Call: Watching—from Sentry to Shepherd of Souls

A second and more immediate event that called Cuthbert to the monastic life in Melrose happened just up the hill from the river, on those purple mountains we'll walk across after we visit the abbey. Cuthbert was tending sheep when it occurred. The connection to biblical motifs is clear enough. Like David, like the good shepherd in Jesus's parable, Cuthbert will become a good shepherd. An upright priest. A holy bishop. A caring father of the North. Cuthbert may indeed have been simply

49

shepherding, but more likely this young warrior of seventeen was not just shepherding, a job typically reserved for the peasant boys he once wrestled with in the mud. It's probable that this shepherding was part of Cuthbert's duty to be on watch amid a military operation. It would make more sense that young Cuthbert was watching as a soldier rather than just a shepherd. That would fit his station and reputation as a warrior, and it is the life he'll renounce to become the shepherd of the souls of the North.

As Cuthbert the sentry watched over sheep in the night, a light moved across the sky, descending to the earth. After a few minutes the light reascended, racing off into the heavens. Late on the night of August 31, 651, Cuthbert had the sense that he had just seen an angel coming to earth to take a soul to heaven. It would later be confirmed that on that very night the great Aiden had died on Lindisfarne. After what Cuthbert had just witnessed, it could no longer be denied or delayed: He was meant not for the battlefield but for the monastery. But as the miracle he had just witnessed in the sky foreshadowed, his duty to be on watch would not come to an end. His call to watch would only pivot toward the divine and renew in earnest, in a deeper and more profound way.

Pastors, priests, and church leaders are called to stay on watch. That is our job, to watch for the actions of the uncontrollable God. To call and attend to our people, reminding them also to stay on watch. Often, we are so caught up with *our own* actions and responsibilities that we forget to watch for the God who acts and calls us to join God's actions in the world. Practicing the countercultural move of watching—anticipatory waiting—makes us available and ready when God calls us to specific actions of ministry. It also makes us ready to receive moments of resonance when they arrive.

Likewise, as parents, watching is an essential element of our calling. We watch over and watch alongside our children, and as we do, we are blessed to live with small people who are much more practiced watchers than we are. Learning to watch for the uncontrollable moments when eternity breaks into the ordinary, and receive those moments alongside our children, shapes us toward the parenting we long for rather than the parenting imposed on us by a culture shaped by grasping for control.

Paying Attention: A Charge for Ordinary Days

God has a surprise for you today.
Watch for it.
And when the day is done,
I will ask you,
What was God's surprise for you?

You will see someone today
who needs kindness.
Watch for them.
And when the day is done,
I will ask you,
Who did you see who needed kindness?

We will live this way,
you and I.
This is how we will live.
Reminding each other to watch,
asking each other what we saw.

We will be noticers,
you and I.
We will be noticers of God.
We will be noticers of other people.
God will surprise us,
people will need kindness,
and we will notice both.

51

We won't know how it will happen,
or when,
but every day it will happen.

We will keep watching
until we trust
that this is true.

And then we will watch
because it is true:
God has a surprise for you today,
every day.
You will see someone who needs kindness today,
every day.

Watching, asking, noticing, remembering,
we will live this way,
you and I.

Trusting God has a surprise for us,
trusting we will see someone who needs kindness
every single, ordinary, holy day.
This is how we will live.

Source: Kara K. Root, *Receiving This Life* (Fortress, 2023), 51.

Witnessing this angel in the sky and knowing he could never be the same, Cuthbert traveled on horseback, spear in hand, down the hill that we will soon go up for our pilgrimage. He headed to the abbey to pray. Cuthbert did not enter the same abbey that we will be visiting shortly. The remains of the abbey that still stand in Melrose are the "new" abbey. It's nothing but ruins now, some eight hundred years old. But it is new in relation to the abbey Cuthbert entered. From the new abbey you can see the river and imagine where the old abbey once sat. The original abbey where Cuthbert arrived in 651 was nearer the River Tweed and at the time was overseen by the great prior Boisil. Boisil was a student of Aiden, who had just died.[1]

When he arrived, Cuthbert dismounted his horse, handing over his reins and spear to a monk, surrendering his warrior watch forevermore. Cuthbert asked to be admitted into Boisil's care as a novice. And so Boisil, the student of the great Aiden, became the teacher (again parallels to Star Wars and Jedi!). Boisil embraced Cuthbert and took him into the old abbey to pray. Relinquishing his roles as shepherd and soldier, Cuthbert stepped into his new vocation—watching over God's people and watching with them for the action of God.

An Unexpected Epithet

Like Cuthbert, we too now move toward the (new) abbey for prayer. While planning for our pilgrimage, we'd told our kids that we'd pray together three times each day of the walk (morning, midday, evening). Kara created a liturgy for each movement of daily prayer, laminated them, and gave each of us a set of cards. The kids protested much less than we imagined they would—really, there was no protest at all. We chalk this up both to their growing maturity and to the influence of Youthfront in Kansas City. For the last five years we'd driven our kids from the high North down to Kansas City's steamy heat for Youthfront's summer camp. We couldn't *not*. Youthfront is overseen by the Boisil of late-modern America—Mike King. King, like no one else, has combined contemporary forms of youth ministry with historical and monastic practices, creating opportunities for young people to learn to pray and serve the triune God by loving the world. Thanks to King and Youthfront, Maisy in particular had been praying the offices for years (at least at camp!). Our daily prayers made sense to them. If summer camp begins the day in prayer, pauses in the middle of the day for prayer, and ends each day with prayer, then we could, too, on this pilgrimage.

It's a beautiful warm and sunny morning in Melrose. The coffee shops and storefronts are swinging open their windows like contented yawns welcoming the new day. Everything feels easy and bright, friendly in every way. As the morning sun hits the (new) abbey, which is just a block or two away, we approach a narrow part of the sidewalk. A building pushes up to the road and the sidewalk disappears, common in a UK village. The building's position reminds everyone that it has existed much longer than the road has. We cross the street to the other side. An older gentleman, walking slowly with his cane, is just feet away from this narrow stretch. We decide to give him room.

Maisy and Andy are a block ahead of Kara and Owen, and they make it to the other side just as a car is coming up the road. There is a woman behind the wheel, all smiles. The sun is glowing off her happy morning face. Just before the street narrows, she honks her horn, and her sunny, cheerful face somehow brightens even more as she waves to someone in their yard. With a *BEEP! BEEP!* and a wave, her actions call out, "Good morning, friend!" The scene has a feeling of resonance, of embracing the world as an open gift. This is the part Andy and Maisy witness. Kara and Owen are higher up the hill, on the other side of the narrow spot. They witness something else.

It just so happens that this happy honk of connection occurs just as the man with the cane is coming to the narrow pass. As the car horn blares behind his back, he assumes it is a direct point of aggression, an angry shout to get his slow self the BEEP! out of the way of the speeding car.

The startled man throws his cane in the air and plasters his anxious body flat against the building in terror. His cane clatters to the pavement and his body presses the wall at nearly every possible point, flattening against the cold morning stone of the building. The woman passes cheerily onward, completely oblivious to the petrified fellow pasted to the wall.

His fright quickly turns to rage toward the source of the aggressive honk, clearly meant to control his location and speed and to demand that he make way for the driver's domineering conquering of the world. As the blissed-out, unaware woman rumbles past, the man steps back from the wall and begins pumping his arm, hand facing her with two fingers up (the UK equivalent to the US middle finger), shattering the quiet of the peaceful morning air by yelling at the top of his lungs, "Bitch!"

This word, reverberating off the stone buildings and echoing around the four of us as we walk, serves as our procession into prayer. We catch up to each other and tell the story from our respective angles. When we've got the whole scene played out before us, we begin to laugh. Not at the man (we understand him) but at the entire scene, the Larry David–esque misunderstanding we just watched unfold: the vast difference between the driver's experience and the man's, and then ours as witnesses who understood the whole moment from both sides. We giggle at being serenaded with profanity as we walk to pray next to an ancient abbey. It's hilarious but fitting that this negative pronouncement commences our holy walk. The way into abundance often begins in absence.

Always a *Via Negativa*

To clearly see truth and beauty, recognizing its texture and detail as a gift, you must spot it against a negative background. You must begin in its absence. Ancient philosophers and theologians called this the *via negativa*. The idea is that to say something true, you must first name all the things you *cannot* say, because all the things that you hope to say are impossible to articulate. For many ancient theologians, the only way to talk about a God who is God, and therefore beyond all knowing, is to speak of what God is not. During the Reformation, Luther adopted and adapted this negative way to remind us that the

Bible (particularly the Pauline epistles) calls us to look for the living God where this God should not be found—on the cross. Luther reminds us to *never* be afraid of the dark. For it is in the dark (in our places of unknowing, in our suffering, in the warped dimensions of our social lives) that we find the possibility of spotting beauty and truth. For Luther, the negativity of the cross unveils the being of God. This unveiling of God's being is marvelously witnessed as love and mercy.

This sensibility finds its way into Rosa, who never dabbles in theology. You would not mistake Rosa for Luther. But as a social theorist, he seems to follow this *via negativa*. Rosa believes that if we're ever to get a handle on the social and cultural conditions that shape us, we must first examine the dark background. We must explore how modernity puts us in conflict with the world around us. He contends that if we're ever going to embrace resonance and welcome uncontrollability, we must first see how and why the forms of action that our society gives to us are so malforming.

Losing Control

After enthusiastically making our way to Melrose Abbey, our budding journey grinds to a sudden halt. The abbey grounds don't open until 10 a.m. Exploring the abbey with the attention it deserves means we won't start our day 1 walk until after 11:30, maybe closer to noon. We don't have many other options, so we assure ourselves that this late start will be just fine. We're actively trying to resist the urge to rush, accomplish, consume this experience. *We only have seven miles to walk this first day. We can easily do that in an afternoon*, we reassure ourselves. It will be our shortest walk until the final day, when we cross to Lindisfarne. Yet, while this first day walk is short, it starts straight uphill, right through the middle of the purple-flocked mountains. For someone living in the Rockies or the Alps these so-called mountains are biggish hills. We know that to our upper Midwestern prairie-land quads, still cramped from tight airplane seats, these hills will be a challenge, so we're feeling the anxiety. It's a struggle to let go and be where we are instead of tackling what's ahead.

We sit in the shadow of the abbey's ancient walls, outside the fence of the cemetery with its crumbling tombstones, waiting for the grounds to open. Doves are cooing and the kids are cranky, but we're easing in. People occasionally walk by with dogs or their own reluctant teenager in tow. We try to be patient, remembering our intention to begin well. *We're close*, we assure each other. *It will start soon.* Kara takes out the morning prayer cards, and we recite our prayers and hold our silence. Then we give each other space.

Finally, the abbey opens. We stroll the abbey grounds listening to the abbey's audio guide. Maisy and Kara find a kids' room with monk costumes. Kara makes a tiny monk from a clothespin and cloth scraps, intending to bring Little Cuthbert along the whole journey. He gets enthusiastically photographed at Melrose Abbey and falls off her pack somewhere before the next stop. (Perhaps a surprise blessing to a fellow pilgrim another day?)

We learn a lot about the abbey and finally make our way back to the road. It's past noon, and obviously Maisy's hungry. There is an annoyingly cheerful sign pointing the way to ice cream, and Maisy's jet lag is heeding its sweet siren song. She asks for ice cream. Then Andy—with full overbearing dad energy—becomes *that guy*. His humor is gone, and his anxiety is spiking. He can't stop looking at his watch.

It's clear that things are getting worse by the second. It's already past noon and we have yet to walk even one step on the pilgrim's route! It's time someone took control here! What is wrong with these people who don't seem to get the urgency of this thing? They are working against our supposedly shared goal! My frustration is absolutely called for. We haven't even located the trailhead! If we don't get going now, it's clear we may never start.

His anxiety buzzing loudly in his head, Andy has turned the corner to anger. The pressing demand for control within him wants the aimless ice cream urges quelled. *Why didn't people make better breakfast choices? The whole world is positioning itself to fight, and I'm here for it!*

It's hard for Andy not to say all these things aloud and spew his frustration all over everyone. It's hard for Kara not to try to control Andy and his anger and reclaim the shared mood she wants everyone on this pilgrimage journey to be committed to experiencing at all times.

The kids withdraw into moody silence. If they could teleport home right now to the closed doors of their bedrooms, no doubt they would. Nobody wants to be with each other at this particular moment. Our aggression has shifted from being directed outside our family to inside. As parents we're ashamed that it has, but it has. We know well these sharp edges and many poky points of aggression. Points of aggression have peppered our parenting and pastoring. We've jumped into them often. Very often. Like the man at the narrow pass, countless times we have felt stuck and attacked, lashing back in fear or defensive anger. Points of aggression and our perceived need for control seem to go together like peanut butter and chocolate— but much less delicious.

Rosa Brings Us to the Point(s)

After Rosa's introduction, filled with the wonder of snow, he claims that the shape of our social and cultural environment forms us to engage the world as points of aggression. The world itself becomes a "point of aggression." This interesting phrase is provocative, but it's also soaked in meaning. The word that jumps out, of course, is "aggression." It's an eye-catching word (more on that below). But its less flashy partner "point" is just as important—particularly regarding parenting and church leadership. It's easy to brush aside "point," leaving it unexamined, because it's familiar. But there is something at stake here. "Point" is a tricky word with many different and distinct meanings. People can use "point" in all sorts of ways. "My point is that dogs are better than cats." "The point of the trip is to drop him off at the university." "The main point of the movie was that human love is fragile." "The insect bit the very point of her nose." "Go down two miles, turn left, and the cabin is on the point." "Actually, let me just point you in the right direction."

By calling our engagement with the world a "point" or "points," we're saying something important about our actions and interactions. Encounter, intersection, and meeting are fundamental to our humanity. Whatever kind of beings we human beings are—particularly whatever kind of parents or church leaders—we are creatures of points. Our actions, our very being in the world, create moments of connection, events of encounter. We are always (and we believe *always*!) living *at* a point and *for* a point.

At a Point—Now and Shared

To be living *at* a point means two things: *now* and *shared*. We are always inside a point of time at a specific place: *now*. A pilgrimage reminds us of this. A pilgrimage is a lifetime in miniature. It reminds us that life is a journey *from*, *toward*, and *for* a point. Pilgrims move from one point in time to the next, from one point in the world to another, giving themselves over in time and attention to an experience they're engaging and a place toward which they're moving.

Parenting and leading people in faith are also pilgrimages. Both make us acutely aware of time and place. And the times we experience are shaped by the places we're in. As parents we say things like, "They were so little when we were on Cannon

Street." "I felt so ready to teach them to read." "I'm lost in these teen years." "Our house feels too small. But I can't bear the thought of him being out of the house next year." "How could those years of footy pajamas and sleepless Christmas Eves be over so soon? They're now gone for good."

Parenting is marked entirely by these movements of time across spaces in which we live out our lives. We somewhat ignore the flows of time in our own lives. But the growing and shifting of our children's lives make our pilgrimage between points of time in distinct spaces poignant and therefore impossible to miss. Our phone or favorite social media platform will even remind us with a pic and a caption, "Remember this, five years ago today?"

In our congregations, the rituals and markers of shared faith keep us aware of the movement of the journey. The liturgical calendar moves us through Advent, Christmas, Lent, Easter, Pentecost, and Ordinary Time over and over again, giving us points of context. "Remember last Christmas Eve, when we streamed the service from our living rooms?" "I love Ash Wednesday. In the paradox of being told to remember I will die, I am reminded how meaningful life is." Burying one another, noticing who is no longer in the choir this Easter, baptizing the child of one of the congregation's children who seemingly just yesterday was confirmed, and didn't she *just* leave for college, like, a minute ago? We see these space and time markers acutely in the lives of those with whom we minister.

In our own aging selves, however, the passing of time shocks us because, though we have been on a journey, we often forget altogether that we are walking it. This may be one reason we have the hardest time staying in the present. A faithful pilgrim must be in the present, praying in the moment, as they move between points. Pilgrimage invites us into the present. To be human is to have a history, to have a past as we move forward in time. And to be human is to anticipate, prepare for, and even dream about a future. Pilgrimages are never aimless walks; they start at a point and move toward a specific destination.

We parents are haunted by our pasts. Either we're horrified or we laugh at the ways we're like our own parents. We worry that our children will make the same mistakes we did. Almost all our anxiety is wrapped up in worries about what kind of future our children will *have*. Worrying about our children's future is not an exclusively modern concern. All people everywhere have done that. What *is* modern is to assume that our children will have a future only if they can win enough resources to make one for themselves. Premodern people believed a good life for their kids was found through obedience and virtue. They longed for their children to find their destiny or fate, but that was outside their own control. Instead, they worried about what kind of people their children would *be*. Our worry is what kind of future our children will *have*. We think that is largely in our own control. For modern people, a good life for our kids is secured by accruing enough resources to live whatever individual dream they want for themselves in the future. It is modern to imagine that our job as parents is to prepare our children to be selves who can win in the game of procuring for themselves a future.

Yet even with these pulls to past and future, ultimately we human creatures can live only right now, right at this point on the trail of our journey. We live in this very point in the present, with its dimensions of time and space that we cannot escape. We can be nowhere else but here at the present. We really can be living only in this moment, in this time, in this right now we're in. We are always *at* a point in time. How we live *at* this point, how we care for these children *at* this point or pastor these people here and now *at* this point, is what matters. It is the only real time and place, the only concrete location of connection with God, ourselves, and these others, who are also present. God is here now and we are here now, even if our minds or hearts struggle to *be here now*.

Gratitude—A Journaling Exercise

One practice for noticing and receiving the world, our lives, God's presence, and each other is gratitude. Gratitude grounds us in the now, and helps us watch for what God is doing, by recognizing what God has done. Here's a journaling exercise for gratitude. (Returning to it and rereading it some months later initiates another round of gratitude and paying attention.)

Psalm 107 summarized: "O give thanks to the Lord, for God is good; for God's steadfast love endures forever. Again and again, when we've cried to the Lord in our trouble, God has saved us from our distress. Let us thank the Lord for God's steadfast love, for God's wonderful works to humankind."

Gratitude Prayer Journaling Exercise

- When I think of the people I call mine, I am thankful for . . .
- When I consider the connections I have in the world (friends, neighbors, coworkers), I am thankful for . . .
- When I think of my body, I am thankful for . . .
- When I reflect on my life in the past few months, I am thankful for . . .
- When I think of things this year that have been painful or challenging, I am thankful for . . .
- When I think of this world, I am thankful for . . .

The second element of living *at* a point is that it is *shared*. Though this point is made by our present (our presence), it is also determined by the presence of others. The trail is always shared. In parenting and leading, there are always others who demand the responsibility of us recognizing that they too have their own distinct moment in the now (which is bound to their own sense of their history and linked to their own dreams for the future). It is not only you who lives *at* a point. You are at a point because you meet others right here. These others are not furniture or extras in *your* moment. They have their own being *at* this same point. What is fully our own present moment is also fully the present moment of others—we meet *at* an axis. Our points have weight not only because they are *ours* but because they are *shared*.

These points also make up the lives of those we are called to love. A parent knows this in their bones. Our children's lives are shaped by the points, moments, they share with us. In these shared points we are compelled to act. The ways we act in these shared points become the shape of our lives, and others' as well. Our lives are the ways we move across time and space from being *at* one point to being *at* the next. To be at a point is to always find yourself in a moment of encounter. We always meet others at the point. We cannot be human without points of shared life, times in which we act, encountering others who share this point in time with us. The pilgrim's trail is walked with others.

Being at shared points gives parenting and church leadership their weightiness. The way we engage shared points has direct impact on others. It powerfully makes the now—which shapes their future and gives coherence to their past—morally good or bad.

Congregations and children look to us to be there for them, to make this point one of support and communion, to help them flourish. In parenting we know that our point in time meets and conditions the point that is also another's. For example, your own midlife, and all its existential tensions, is also your kid's childhood. How you respond (act) to being at the point of middle life will shape their childhood. These points are fused because both of you meet *at* this time. You both have your mutual humanity right here. These shared points occur in church leadership as well; your words of teaching or acts of listening meet someone in a specific place and time in their life. How you are living at the moment, the point at which you meet others—whether you're at a point of deepened learning, personal frustration with God, or considering retirement—is shaped by where you and they both are in this moment.

To act *at* this point can become about control, or it can become a place to encounter the uncontrollable. It can be a point of aggression or a point of communion. The honking woman and mobility-challenged man met *at* a point. As human beings locked always at a point, they illustrate how we meet the point as either a moment of tense aggression or a moment of shared connection. Either "life's a bitch" or it's filled with misunderstood longing.

In both parenting and church leadership, we too often meet this moment seeking control. We're too worried about the future, too caught up living out of narratives of the past, to be in *this* moment, to be at *this* point, to be where our bodies are. Unable to be on the trail of the now, and yet simultaneously always stuck in the now, we find that control becomes the shape of our actions. Out of fear, not necessarily of the moment itself but of what could be lost or of what could go wrong, we seek to control our kids' and our church's (and *the* church's) futures. We make this moment, this now, a point of control due to fear.

Of course, we don't mean to do any of this. Our grasping for control is rarely a conscious choice. It's instinctual. Our modern lives mold us for the kind of action that seeks control. To show how we're shaped for this control, we'll have to start unpacking "aggression." But before we get there, we first need to explore one other element of *point*.

For a Point—Growth Mindset

To be human is to be living *at* a point, but it is also to be living *for* a point. We are compelled to act because we live *at* a point with others, but how we act is determined by the point *for which* we're living. The proverbial beach bum tells us it's easy to live in the point we're *at*. "You just flow into the now, man. Don't think about anything but the now, man." But he

64

usually has nobody he's responsible for. Scratch the surface and we quickly see not a sun-soaked sage but a narcissistic dud. He lives in the now but not as a shared point with others in that now, bound in confession and commitment. He lives in the now only for himself. Living responsibly *at* a point with others necessarily means living *for* a point. This living for a point demands some embrace (or at least awareness) of the past and future, even as we live in the now. Pilgrimages force us to stay in the now but also force us to recognize that we are on the present trail holding the prayers of our past and led forward toward the holy place to which our journey points.

This living *for* a point is central to the thought of Hartmut Rosa (something he takes from Charles Taylor). All human beings' actions are directly shaped by our sense of the good life. We human beings are always living *for* some tacit or explicit purpose and out of some sense of meaning. Through our experience of the past and our hope for the future, we have some sense that there is a *point* to our present points of encounter. We are creatures bound in the now who never live in that now without wanting that now to be *for* a larger point. We always want the now to be good and full of purpose and meaning. Whether implicitly or explicitly (whether we're in touch with it or not), our understanding of "good" and "meaning" is shaped into a story that draws from our experiences of the past and our longings for the future. Our actions are always fueled by a story. The story we tell ourselves in the now shapes the way we engage our points of encounter. Parenting and church leadership always happen in the now. Even so, they can never be done faithfully without a story of what the point we're *at* is *for*.

The problem is that the stories we hold—which directly shape our points—are so often given to us by the society and culture in which we live. Most of the stories that fundamentally shape us happen behind our back. We internalize

65

these stories without hardly noticing, and yet they shape us momentously, particularly when it comes to parenting and leading in the church. Our definition of a good parent or a good church leader comes on the winds of the stories that shape our cultural life. We support our stories with actions, such as meeting with every teacher to ensure they understand our child's individual perspective, nipping all church discontent in the bud, making sure our kid gets the playing time they deserve on the team, or ensuring that the church council understands how much time we've put into the job. Yet we often don't notice the many ways these stories form us, determining our actions.

These cultural stories, with their weighty moral definitions of what is good, assert that the best action seeks and exerts control. Modernity assumes that if the now is to be good, it must be controlled. Through technology and organization, modernity takes sweeping steps to control nature, social interactions, and even our individual attention and emotions. The pursuit of control has become so extensive that we never even doubt it. Many of us now shrug our shoulders when told that companies are harvesting our data and eroding our social connections, because in return we receive control in shopping and transportation. As long as we *get* some control for *giving up* control of our data and privacy, we're cool. The point of life and the point of all our encounters is *control*.

Naturally, it's assumed that control makes for a good parent and a good leader. The goal of gaining and expanding control is deemed worthy of our ambition; it is even our *responsibility*. We come to accept that the points we're *at* need to be controlled *for* a larger point.

What is this larger point? That's where things get a little tricky. The point is not necessarily control itself. We obsess about control but not because control is our real objective. Control for control's sake is not a captivating story. Sure, our

66

actions are molded for control, but not because what we ultimately want is control. Few parents or church leaders would name control as their ambition. (At least, not without shame and derision.) We know that "being controlling" is not necessarily good. Even so, control becomes necessary and therefore the shape of our action because of what we ultimately desire.

What comes on the winds of these formative cultural stories tells us the point is *growth*. Whether or not we would say it this way, what we've come to believe is that all the points we are *at* are *for* growth. The stories of a good life, a good parent, and a good pastor all revolve around a constant need for *more and more growth*. Just go with us here, and you'll see what we mean. Growth talk is everywhere, from wellness culture advice on how we should eat and exercise to theories on economic expansion or church health and more. The ancients feared evil or demons. We moderns fear the loss of growth in our children or churches. Our modern society, and modern people in it, shapes our lives toward attaining more—more money, more stability, more experiences, more resources, more acknowledgment, more affirmation. We assume that the now is *for* growth into a future of more growth.

Within such a paradigm, parenting is for growing children— and not strictly biologically or morally—as selves who can win more and more growth for themselves in the future. Good parenting is giving your kids the resources to grow into their dreams, even grow bigger dreams. Church leadership exists to grow as well. But that aim is not always to grow persons into the person of Jesus Christ, who died and was resurrected beyond growth in the glory of eternity. Instead, churches aim to grow their size and impact through programs and initiatives. Ultimately the obsession becomes to grow large enough to not lose or waste the limited resources the congregation does possess.

In modernity, the opposite of growth is death. We desire growth for our children and our churches because modernity tells us that things that don't grow—quickly and exponentially—are bound for destruction. Our story of the need for growth is written as a morality tale of warning more than a narrative of glory. If we don't take control, our children or our congregation will fall behind. Without growth they'll never have the buoyancy to reach a future point of being good. They must grow or die. It feels dire and terrifying, but fear is a powerful motivator. On the other hand, the counterforming practices of sabbath rest and pilgrimage walking are ways to practice nongrowth, nonachievement—surrendering control in the practice of dying. In a pilgrimage, we die on the trail as we move not toward growth but toward the places where God's glory shines.

The compulsion for continuous growth makes control seem necessary. Since we are always grasping after growth, control becomes obligatory. We are naive if we think growth could be achieved without control. Look at everyone else seeking growth as the point of their lives! Modernity assures us that control is the only way to get to growth and thus fend off death. If we don't take control, growth will be lost. Our very lives will be lost. Without growth we are irrelevant, left behind, extraneous. Our lives are meaningless and our futures aimless. Again, we might not necessarily think of our aim as growth—especially in parenting. We see our goal as giving our kids opportunities, expanding their options, increasing their resources, and widening their possibilities. A life of limited opportunity, few options, scarce resources, and restricted possibilities means no future at all. We *must* seek control because other parents are preparing their children to grow past our kid, achieving and possessing the dream that would make our child happy.

Church leaders feel the pressure that comes from the awareness that other churches with better programs are growing larger, attracting our people away from our congregation. That church's growth means our church is shrinking—we had better get some control before it's too late. We need more control to keep our children or congregation from falling behind. Behind what? Behind more growth.

Perpetual growth demands control. Increase or die. And now that our actions are shaped by control, our points of encounter (the *at*) and purpose (the *for*) become hurried and aggressive. There is too much at stake and no time or energy to waste.

Getting Aggressive with Rosa (for Growth)

Rosa wants us to see that our points of contact with the world are first and foremost points of aggression. We assume that all our points of contact will be aggressive, and so we respond with aggression. Now, we don't take pleasure in destruction or make aggression our sport, like raiding Vikings. Few of us are looking for a fight. But we always seem to find one because we concede that the point is to get control so we can get growth, so we can avoid wasting or losing our lives. If we have control at each point, we will grow and therefore live well. We will achieve a good life. But control and its accompanying growth must be attained; it must be won. There is only so much to go around; another's gain is our loss. Control must be wrested loose from the hands of others or from the mystery of uncontrollability. Life (and parenting and pastoring) becomes no longer a shared pilgrimage but a constant battle. Fear of decline and pursuit of growth demands a life of throwing elbows instead of joining hands, making life (in all its points) an aggressive competition.

We are shaped, and thus compelled, like a reflex, to yell back at the world, "Bitch!" In many ways this is what it means to be modern (at least late modern). We're led to assume that life mostly is a bitch. That slogan is a shorthand story that encompasses a community's or even a society's moral vision. In theology, slogans are shorthand for doctrines. Luther's slogan "justification by faith alone" is the shorthand story of a rich and detailed claim about reality. It's no wonder "Life's a bitch" is an enduring late-modern slogan, appearing at the end of the twentieth century. It's the story, the doctrine, of the moral shape of our embattled life. It voices the fact that life is made up of points of aggression, and it communicates something significant in its crassness. Some of us remember when that slogan appeared on bumper stickers and T-shirts, becoming part of popular culture in the 1980s and '90s. Cheap, disposable consumer goods were the perfect landing place for this slogan because neoliberal capitalism and its hyperconsumerism had just doubled down on competition for the sake of all-out economic growth. The whole economy, and society with it, turned ferociously toward maximum competition. After all, growth had slowed. And without growth, every part of our lives would be in crisis—at least, that's what we were told. Life is a point of aggression ("Life's a bitch") because competition has spilled into all the cracks and crevices of our lives. Everything is about wins or losses—get control so you can grow your wins and mitigate your losses.

On that peaceful Melrose morning, with the rising sun illuminating the abbey, the well-meaning driver was actually honking as a point of *connection*, a point of greeting, even a point of welcome. The surprised and upset man—likely for good reasons embedded in his past—could meet the moment only as a point of aggression. He probably did not assume that the woman hated him. It was just that her perceived need for control turned him into an object. He feared he would be run over. When we are but soldiers in a competitive battle for personal growth, the slow are roadkill. When control becomes the shape of the good life, all our encounters are turned into objectified points of aggression. We objectify each other. All our relationships—even with our own children and congregations—become instrumentalized. They become tools for growth.

Turning all our encounters into points of aggression may be (somewhat) tenable in business, and perhaps less so in politics (welcome to the American political scene, where opponents refuse even to talk to each other). But such points of aggression are diabolical, and pure cancer, in the family and in the church. When our relations with our children or within our congregations are turned into instruments for growth, we lose something fundamental. We no longer function together on a pilgrim way, seeking the now to be filled with prayer, our tomorrows bursting with encounters with the living God, and our pasts redeemed by the mercy of God's Son. Because of the pressing call for control and our fear of losing growth and falling irredeemably behind, aggression has burrowed its way into how we modern people parent and how we function in congregations.

Entering the Uncontrollable

At the very point of starting out on St. Cuthbert's Way, we pilgrims have lit into a point of aggression. Even before we set foot on the actual path, our journey has turned from a pilgrimage into a forced march. "We're late. No ice cream!" Andy bellows. Feeling the day getting away from us, Andy reaches for control, falling back into a growth and pursuit frame of mind. There is nothing pressing, no goal to achieve, no race to win. All we need to do is walk, just be, aiming our fragile bodies toward God's holy island. Yet we are finding it hard to meet this point in any other way than with aggression.

But a pilgrimage is entering the uncontrollable, giving yourself over to being on the trail, only that. With aggression still pulsing through our veins and restrained animosity festering between us, we make our way back up the hill, past the now infamous narrow spot, and through the quaint town. We stride so quickly ahead that we miss our first arrow marker that would take us off the road and onto St. Cuthbert's Way. We have to backtrack. We are spaced out several meters apart. Crabby and defensive, nobody wants to be with anyone else. Finally, Maisy notices the spot: a narrow walkway between a fence and a building with the Cuthbert cross silently displayed, inviting us onto a different path. We regroup, take a breath, and step off the road and onto the trail.

We begin to climb up the Eildon Hills, the tops covered in merry purple flowers due to ancient volcanoes bringing a different ecosystem here than in the valley below. As we climb, we feel the aggression begin to dissipate, leached out of us by the hot sun. Our legs burn. The view keeps getting more spectacular. The anticipation of the journey returns. We feel the joy of finding the next trail marker and calling out to each other. The tension between us disappears and we are present, sharing the now with these others we love. Maisy's camera comes out, and she begins seeing the beauty through her lens. Owen finds his inner motor and plows purposefully forward, thrilling to the movement and the vistas. We pause and let one another catch up from time to time. As we thread our way between North Eildon and Mid Hill, Owen wants to climb to the top of it, so Kara joins him. When they reach the peak, they discover a cairn there and add their own rocks to the pile created by waves of previous pilgrims.

We've begun. We are doing this thing we've been planning forever. We are together here in the Scottish Borderlands. We are here, now, present in a shared moment. We pause to take long swigs from our water bottles and gaze back at tiny Melrose far below. It was here that Cuthbert on watch saw angels taking Aiden's body into heaven from the far distant island to which we journey. We are in these same mountains, covered in late summer's purple flowers.

In the name of the sending Father,
in the name of the pilgrim Son,
in the name of the wind-like Spirit,
in the name of the Three in One.

CALL TO WORSHIP

Let the beauty of the Lord look upon us.
Guide the way of our feet,
guide the way of our feet.
Amen.

PSALM READING: PSALM 121

I lift up my eyes to the hills—
    from where will my help come?
My help comes from the LORD,
    who made heaven and earth.

He will not let your foot be moved;
    he who keeps you will not slumber.
He who keeps Israel
    will neither slumber nor sleep.

The LORD is your keeper;
    the LORD is your shade at your right hand.

The sun shall not strike you by day,
nor the moon by night.

The LORD will keep you from all evil;
he will keep your life.
The LORD will keep
your going out and your coming in
from this time on and forevermore.

SILENCE

THE LORD'S PRAYER

Our Father, who art in heaven,
Hallowed be your name,
Your kingdom come,
Your will be done,
On earth as it is in heaven.
Give us this day our daily bread,
And forgive us our trespasses,
As we forgive those who trespass against us.
Lead us not into temptation,
But deliver us from evil,
For yours is the kingdom, and the power,
and the glory, forever and ever. Amen.

BENEDICTION

Blessing of discovery be ours,
and blessing of rest.
Blessing of scenery be ours,
and blessing of saints.
Blessing of meeting be ours,
and blessing of quiet.
Blessing of friendship be ours,
and blessing of God.

——— CLOSING PRAYER ———

God be with us at every leap.
Christ be with us on every steep.
Spirit be with us in every deep.
Each step of the journey we go. Amen.

——— WALKING PRAYER ———

Christ behind,
Christ before,
Christ beside.

Christ below,
Christ above,
Christ within.

Source: Morning prayer compiled by Kara K. Root. Portions adapted from Ray Simpson, "Common Prayer from the Community of Aidan and Hilda," 446, 450, https://www.raysimpson.org/userfiles/file/CAH_Common_Prayer __Committee_7__April_2017_updated.pdf. Used with permission.

4

Grow, Grow, Grow

A Margarita on Purple Mountains

There are two constants on the trail. The first is that Owen is always out ahead, sometimes as much as a quarter mile. He eventually stops and waits for us. But his pace is always steadier than the rest of ours. This feels like a miracle. When we planned the pilgrimage, in the middle of the pandemic when his life was entirely sedentary, we had concerns about Owen's capacity to keep up and keep going. But his transformation over the past nine months came through walking. Now he's our leader. We're being pulled along in Owen's steady, confident wake. We're releasing him to go at his own speed. We both have a hard time with this; we keep resisting the urge to tell him to slow down and walk with us. But when we let go, we marvel at his pace. It's impressive.

The second constant is that Owen always has at least one earbud in. He's always listening to something. At first this bugs us—immensely. We want him to be present, to be *at* this point, to be in the now. We want to control how he's experiencing the pilgrimage because we fear whatever he's listening to is allowing him to escape this moment. We worry he's missing it. We want to make him put away the headphones (maybe even throw his phone off the mountain). But this, no doubt, would become a point of aggression. And by the time we make it to the top of the purple mountains, we get it. Looking out on Melrose from the location of Cuthbert's sheep watch makes Andy think of a song.

There's an obscure indie band called Purple Mountains. We're not the kind of people who can flex our knowledge of obscure indie bands. (Maybe TV shows, but not bands.) We're the kind of people who love Coldplay (we can feel your hate, and shame on you!). And we'll never stop listening to the Counting Crows. No, it was someone much cooler than us who called Andy's attention to Purple Mountains: Matt Thompson from Hamilton, Ontario. After reading something Andy wrote, Matt emailed a link to a Purple Mountains song called "Margaritas at the Mall." Andy's been using it in presentations ever since.

As we make it to the top of the purple mountains in the Borderlands of Scotland, Andy starts humming "Margaritas at the Mall." It's a catchy tune. (We dare you to YouTube it. You'll be humming it the rest of the day. More than likely, it will get stuck in your head for the next week or two. That's a warning.) But more than catchy, the song features some insightful and haunting lyrics. Cuthbert would not be able to make heads or tails of these lyrics. If Owen's phone and earbuds somehow fell through a wormhole and landed next to Cuthbert on these same purple mountains in AD 651, he would . . . well, he would have no idea what to do with them. But if the phone happened to be playing "Margaritas at the Mall" and he was able to listen, Cuthbert would have the hardest time making sense of it. And not just because he'd have no clue what a mall is—or a margarita, unfortunately. More so because the longings of the lyrics are so (late) modern, so much about coping with a world made controllable.

Thanks to copyright law, we can give you only a very small taste (a sip, shall we say) of these lyrics. To fully drink in the song, you really will have to YouTube it. The first thing to know as you do is that the writer and singer of these lyrics is David Berman, who is better known as an avant-garde poet. He is not connected to a faith community. This song has no element of being an apologetic for any religious system or worldview. Rather, it comes from the mind of a man who long ago gave up on such belief. He moved past any sense that there is a God or any transcendent force in the world. Yet, having done so— having accepted that existence is only material and natural, basically pointless—he's left choking on its sugary meaning-lessness, coughing up the flatness of it all. He's left, surprisingly and shockingly, deadened by the vapidness. Having accepted this shallow existence as a good life, he now wonders whether Western society's pushing of God to the far edges of our lives has had the consequence of making our lives nearly pointless, like having margaritas at the mall.

To Berman, margaritas represent a safe and easily control-lable pleasure that occupies the soul but leaves it tipsy, dull, and ultimately impoverished. Lost are the horizons of signifi-cance. Lost are transcendent visions of angels descending to earth. Lost are pilgrimages into the uncontrollable. Instead, we've enclosed ourselves in consumer prisons. The mall, where we consume and gratify, is the anti-pilgrimage. It's a no-place place, everywhere and nowhere at the same time. Inside a mall we lose all sense of being somewhere, even of light and dark-ness. Malls demand little (but your money) and offer even less. But we don't notice that we're inside a self-imposed jail because our senses are overtaken by menial pleasures. (This may be the point where some of us who avoid actual malls realize that our phones have become the mall.)

We've traded the ambiguity of the here and now for a no-place place of browsing because we've wanted a world that we can control. We've wanted a world where our actions can bring growth upon growth, so we turn from depth and replace it with an incredible surplus of variety, as though variety could replace depth. The margaritas come in assorted colors and flavors, even acid green and peacock blue, as Berman's chorus repeats again and again. But this incredible variety—this controllable life inside the air-conditioned, perfume-scented mall—has strangled the human spirit with controllable banality. Control demands reduction. Optimization diminishes the dimensions of the world.

Here are just two lines from the song, coming to the listener as questions:

> How long can the world go on under such a subtle God?
> How long can the world go on with no new word from God?

He then painfully tells us we have no answer to these questions—modernity has supposedly outgrown them. But this has left him listless and empty, salt-parched and tipsy on tequila. What we have instead of the weight of Cuthbert's God, who acts and moves in history, is . . . well . . . margaritas at the mall. It's what all this control for the sake of growth adds up to after all.

All we have now are many pleasures and safe harbors from divine consequence and the thought of eternal punishment. The god of the mall is not an uncontrollable force met in the wild of the pilgrim's way. Berman is beginning to see that these pleasures are not worth living for. These safe harbors, though calm and a bright turquoise blue, are poison to the soul. Berman's song essentially asks, *Doesn't all this control—which even encourages us to have no ears for a speaking God, promising us growth upon growth—in the end give us just a hollowness, a malaise of meaninglessness?*

Berman's own answer is clear and tragic. His lyrics poignantly say so. But also, heartbreakingly, during the pandemic, just months after releasing this song and album, Berman killed himself. A world seeking to eviscerate all uncontrollability for the sake of growth, where even the uncontrollable God is silenced by our distractions, has its consequences. Ironically, a world made safe and controllable like a mall becomes dangerous to the human spirit. As Rosa has shown, this pursuit of growth by control makes our very selves a point of aggression. Growth by control has deep mental-health consequences. We've seen this with our own children. The need for constant growth creates anxiety. To combat our anxiety, we try to get a firmer grip on life, seeking more and more control, which only creates more anxiety. When we get too tired to keep our grip on control, our anxiety slides into despondency—into depression. This, in turn, only seems to further make the self a point of aggression, because we believe the only way out of our depression is to find a way back into control. We seek to medicate our anxiety or depression with more control so we can get back to chasing more growth—which was the problem to begin with. Seeking control, believing that control stabilizes us, forces us deep into a rut, keeping us racing around the circle as long as we can keep it up. Tragically, for some people, the last, desperate grasp for control is to seek to escape the merciless circle once and for all.

Dynamic Stabilization for Growth

This frantic circle of chasing more growth with more control is hard to break, the deep rut difficult to escape. We cannot see that the snake is eating its tail. We often can't recognize that the control that begets growth for the sake of more growth only makes us exhausted and anxious for more control. We don't want to lose the growth we've gained. This is a vicious circle that only mall muzak and happy hour, half-price margaritas (or online

81

shopping deals and entertaining TikToks) can make livable. This happy hour has us in its clutches. We don't see the circle because it is so fundamental to the DNA of a modern society. Like a fish that doesn't know it's in water, we modern people have come to assume that the anxious circle is just the way things are, even as it crushes our soul. We feel uneasy, but as modern people we tell ourselves that such discontent must be *within us*. The discontent is caused by *our own* failures to keep up. The problem is not the system; it is *our* performance. It couldn't possibly be that the water we swim in is polluted, right? We need soul-sick poets to point out the contexture of this deeper truth.

While Rosa is not a poet, he does draw from the poetic to perceptively point out not only why this circle exists but why we assume it is necessary and why it seems to force us to go faster and faster. Our increasing speed only deepens the rut, thereby making the circle more dangerous to our soul with every revolution (rendering us and our encounters with the world more aggressive). Rosa says, "A modern society, as I define it, is one that can stabilize itself only dynamically, in other words one that requires constant economic growth, technological acceleration, and cultural innovation in order to maintain its institutional status quo."[1]

Let that profound statement sink in.

What makes a modern society modern is that it stabilizes itself by growth, and then by more growth on top of more growth. Growth is not just a wish, a hoped-for outcome, or a by-product of some other good. It is the *only* good. Growth is an ultimate necessity. Growth is not something that just happens; it is the very (often the only) point to modern life. Growth *can't be opted out of.*

A modern society obsesses over growth but not for the sake of greed (though modern societies do create many greedy people). Rather, we *need* growth, and more each year, to maintain the status quo. In order to not fall tragically, fatally behind, there must be a constant reaching for growth—even to just stay in the same place! Growth demands our complete attention. And those who refuse growth put us all at risk.

Rosa uses the academic-heavy term "dynamic stabilization" to describe this reality. Modern life is stable enough to be dependable *only* when it is growing—when it is vigorously seeking more growth, like a swarm of locusts. Modern life requires constant motion. The purpose of this constant motion is not divine communion or purpose, ritual or tradition, not even something beautiful or true, but just more growth on top of more growth. More money, more reach, more experiences, more recognition, more love and acceptance for our weary selves— modern humans in modern societies need *more*. More winning and more growth. But again, this growth isn't intended to put us ahead; we need growth just to keep from falling behind. We must go faster and faster so we don't lose what ground we have.

In modern societies, things and people are dependable only when they have control over the future, assuring themselves of a future of growth. If a country's standard of living is to continue, its GDP must grow. If a company is to stay in business, its profits must grow beyond 10 percent (2 to 3 percent is not enough to stabilize it). If a congregation or denomination is to stay open and functioning, it must grow. To achieve the growth it is lacking, a church must innovate—this is the only way it can stabilize itself and have a future. If our own children are to live their dreams and have a good life, even maintain the standard of living they grew up with, we must anxiously hurry them to grow their activity involvement, increase their test scores, and raise their overall ability to succeed. A stable future is not a given. It must be grasped. Without dynamic actions to grow resources, abilities, and options, our children's prospects for a good life could be lost.

Rosa says it like this: "In terms of cultural perception, this escalatory perspective has gradually turned from a promise into a threat. Growth, acceleration, and innovation no longer seem to assure us that life will always get better; they have come instead to be seen as an apocalyptic, claustrophobic menace."[2]

No wonder we need control! We need to control for the sake of future growth, because otherwise in our wake will come a destructive loss, a painful falling behind, and a dismal future. No wonder anxiety and depression proliferate in our late-modern societies. We so badly want to protect our children and congregations from this bleak outcome, and our only option is to pursue growth by seeking more and more control.

If such apocalyptic thoughts of a calamitous future without growth seem far-fetched to you, Rosa adds, "If we fail to be better, faster, more creative, more efficient, and so on, we will lose our jobs, businesses will close, tax revenues will decline while expenditures increase, there will be budget crises, we won't be able to maintain our healthcare system, our pension levels, and our cultural institutions, the scope of potential political action will grow ever narrower, and in the end the entire political system will appear to have lost its legitimacy."[3] All this will happen quickly unless we maintain growth upon growth.

No wonder we need margaritas (and Netflix) to medicate us! Inside the habitat of this anxious circle, the ground we live on becomes lifeless and hollowed out by the need for control to win growth. We can never stop to be encountered, never just receive or just be. When we stop, we're meant to feel guilty, like we're wasting time, needing even such experiences to be optimized for more growth ("I play pickleball so I can deal with stress at work," "I sleep eight hours to build up my immune system, so I don't get sick and have to cancel a business trip," "I play with my kids because it produces positive self-image and confidence that will allow them to succeed in life").

Up against the loud buzz of growth, we become unable to hear the uncontrollable God speak. We've developed a distaste, even disgust, for uncontrollability. We can't hear God because, again to draw from Berman's song, modern life has made God so very subtle. God has been made controllable. Growth has become our true and only salvation, and so we can't tolerate an *interrupting* God, a wild God of uncontrollability, who has no mind for growth.

God of the Cross

Growth has become our god. So naturally, we have little patience for God's doddering church that seems fundamentally uninterested in—even uninformed about and unmotivated by—growth. We feel the need to bring the church up to speed to keep it relevant. We moderns choose the mall and its margaritas over the uncontrollable Word of God, over a life of uncontrollable encounters that might draw us into stopping and receiving, and over a community of souls pointed toward the uncontrollable. Of course, modernity, particularly in its American form, is not absent "God." Modernity is not atheistic in that way. Churches are still open, and people still like to say they're praying when a public tragedy occurs. But this modern, subtle "God" is only an idea that helps us in our battles for winning growth. This "God" is ultimately under our control. The social media accounts of professional athletes and the media empires of prosperity preachers are the most visible witnesses of such a subtle "God."

But the wild God of Israel, made known in Jesus Christ crucified, has little concern for growth. We know that will shake some of you, our readers, but we mean it. As a matter of fact, this God, who is anything but subtle, works in the *opposite* direction of growth. Jesus tells us in a parable that God is like a shepherd who leaves the ninety-nine sheep to find the one that is lost (Matt. 18). The wild, uncontrollable God made known in Jesus Christ finds the *one*—encounters the *one*—because the one is more valuable than the economic growth of the ninety-nine. A God who believes that the one lost sheep is greater than the ninety-nine is a God who meets us not as a point of aggression but in and through encounters of mercy and confession.

What stabilizes the kingdom of God is not growth but the very person of Jesus Christ, who seeks and finds the lost to embrace and be with this one, and who dies by the aggressive hands of control so that we might commune completely with this uncontrollable God.

But Jesus's 1 > 99 doesn't sit well with us. Instead, we're tempted to make God into an idol of growth, into a fertility god, into a Baal that the God of Israel called the Israelites to leave behind long ago. The gods of growth cannot save; Israel forgets and relearns that repeatedly. The gods of growth can only give you malls and margaritas as appeasement for endless toil with no sabbath, no rest. Only the God who arrives to encounter the lost one, who faces death and impossibility, can save. But to recognize this saving does not require that you *do more*. Instead, you must rest and accept this uncontrollability. You must confess that this God of Israel is no Baal, no fertility god of growth. You must seek this God's working, which comes in hidden ways that are opposite to dominating growth and control. So hidden and opposite that this God of Israel ultimately comes to us defeated and pushed out of the world on the cross.

The power of the cross, the weapon of Roman control, is broken not by the battle for control but by surrender. The cross, the nefarious instrument of control, is transformed into a portal of ultimate uncontrollability. God turns the cross into the uncontrollable mystery of salvation—life coming from death. Modernity's dynamic stabilization and its worship of control for the sake of growth often make us unable to see life as an uncontrollable pilgrimage in which we seek to encounter the uncontrollable humanity of others and God. We miss the presence of our children calling us to walk with them and the privilege of journeying with a congregation into God's uncontrollable calling.

How to Control the World

We make the world controllable in many ways, but all our attempts at control share four elements or dimensions, according to Rosa. These four dimensions encapsulate what David Berman sensed in the Purple Mountains song.

Make It Visible

Rosa says that "making the world controllable means, first, making it *visible*, that is, making it knowable."⁴ Night vision accessories, doorbell cameras, super telescopes, and full-body MRIs—we reach to see what we otherwise cannot see, losing the mystery of the world. Rejecting any mystery that might be uncontrollably loose in the world, we no longer live knowing that the wild God is always before us. "To trod the ground of visible" is to walk its dusty paths or "glittering billboards," as Berman sings. What matters in such a controllable world is what can be *seen* and therefore possessed.

Make It Reachable

Rosa's second dimension of controllability is that the world must be made *reachable* or *accessible*. The far reaches of space, the deepest layers of the earth's crust, the inner working of our cells—we create the means to make every part of the world accessible. This desire to make the world reachable starts with the best intentions. Like a four-year-old with a baby bird, having reached the world, we are moved by it. But desiring to continue to be moved by the world, we seek to control the world, holding it firmer and tighter in our sweaty palm. We're frightened to loosen our grip, fearing that the world will fly away, becoming too unreachable to fulfill our desires. We start by being moved by the uncontrollability of the world, but tragically we cage (with technological bars) the uncontrollability of the world with our controllable accessibility. These two dimensions of the *visible* and the *reachable* necessitate the final two dimensions of controllability, which relate most directly to the ways we parent and how we lead in the church.

Make It Manageable

The third dimension of bringing the world under control is making it *manageable*. "Innovation" is such an exciting word for us late moderns because it's a form of management that brings elements of uncontrollability under our control. Uber brings the uncontrollability of cabs into the control of the consumer by managing the location of drivers and riders through an app. The app also manages payments (as technology is the ultimate manager of the world). The world is made reachable, and presumably visible, by the pursuits of management. The best managers take the guesswork out of access, leading us to growth through control.

Good late-modern parenting becomes, at its core, a form of management. Maybe in one sense parenting has always been that. But now the parents' job is to manage the world so that their child, without risk, can advance and achieve. The "best" parents manage their children's lives, diving headlong into their children's schools, to ensure all is running smoothly. We complain about our children's school. We parents often believe the school is being mismanaged, which puts our child at risk in the race for the growth of advancement (or we just want to help make the school better by *assisting* the management). Parents know the school is being mismanaged, because management is at the core of our own parenting practice. We, as parents, first and foremost imagine ourselves as managers. Any mismanagement feels like a deep threat to our children's future, putting at risk our children's ability to grow and advance. Poor management fails to give the child a complete system of control that can assure growth. We fill our homes with chore charts, share calendars on our digital devices, and use location trackers, task minders, preset reminders, and alarms to optimize our families' lives.

Of course, church leadership too becomes about management in the drive for control and growth. Just as the "best" parents are managers, growing their children's access to resources and activities, the "best" church leaders are managers too. When the main issue the church faces is (not the Word of the unreachable mystery of God but) a lack of growth, then the pastor must become a manager. And when the pastor becomes a manager, God inevitably becomes subtle, because God must be controlled. God, too, must be managed. This managing of God takes on another wrinkle that moves us into the fourth dimension of controllability.

Make It Useful

When the church leader (or even a parent) is a manager, all things must be useful. *Usefulness* is the fourth dimension of making the world controllable. Inside a controllable world where everything that matters is *visible*, *reachable*, and *manageable*, only directly *useful* things are welcome. We have little time for a ritual or practice that cannot be justified by some direct usefulness—it lowers stress, it works your abs, it prepares you for what's next, on and on it goes. When our pursuit is to control the world so we can achieve growth in all ways, all pastoral practice must be first and foremost useful. The sermon ceases to be about opening the mysteries of the uncontrollable God moving in the uncontrollable world. Instead, the sermon gives the listener useful advice on how to use spirituality to control the world. Worship and singing together are justified activities if we can explain how they lower stress and attract new members to help us grow. The creeds become pointless, because they aren't very useful, are they? Certainly not in a modern world where growth is our necessity. Theology, too, becomes only an appendix to pastoral practice because its attention is on the uncontrollable, unmanageable, and unreachable God. What isn't useful has no value in making the world controllable.

When reviewing Cuthbert's life, we see there is little that Bede records about usefulness. Almost all of Bede's stories are about invisible wonders made manifest. Almost none are about Cuthbert's useful management. Surely Cuthbert did some useful managing as bishop, but Bede finds no reason to record that. What is worth recording are the times of prayer when the uncontrollable came near, blessing Cuthbert with care and mercy. For instance, Bede tells us two stories involving Cuthbert and food. There is little that is useful and manageable here. There is no sustainable food program, just one-off meals. But these meals come uncontrollably. Actually, the agency of animals is essential to these stories.

In one tale Cuthbert is traveling and starving. He stops to pray at a little abandoned hut. As he prays, his horse goes to a thatched roof and begins pulling down the straw. Falling to the ground, wrapped in cloth, is a warm half loaf of bread and a little meat. Just enough for one

Cuthbert's horse finding food on the roof

meal. The reader is left to assume that this one meal of bread and meat was placed there by an angel.

In another tale, Cuthbert and a young companion are on the trail near the Tweed River. They are starving, with no prospects for provisions. Cuthbert and the young companion pray for food. An eagle dives into the river, pulls a fish from the water, and drops it at Cuthbert's feet. After praising God, Cuthbert tells his young companion to prepare the fish, and he says that the bird has ministered to them, so in thanks the eagle should be given back half the fish. Cuthbert feels no need to manage the miracle by growing it. There is no sense that feeding the eagle will influence the eagle to keep working for them. Rather, Cuthbert receives a gift from the uncontrollable world, from the eagle who obeyed the uncontrollable God. Cuthbert's response is to return the gift with a gift, keeping him squarely in an uncontrollable world, encountering not a subtle but a wild God who sends eagles and angels to feed God's servants.

Cuthbert and the eagle

Liturgy of the Cell Phone

One of the most powerful practices to shift from controlling time to receiving time in sabbath rest is to disconnect from the cell phone. Cell phones have become the ultimate talisman of control—our go-to tool for making the world visible, reachable, manageable, and useful. Forgetting a cell phone on a drive feels downright dangerous.

91

Being inaccessible in case of a crisis is utterly irresponsible. Turning it off for any length of time feels nearly impossible. Several years ago, a friend reached out to Kara in frustration at all the cell phone distractions in work meetings, asking if she knew of anything to help people collectively hang up the phone and instead talk to the people they are with. Not finding anything, Kara wrote this. It has become a staple in our congregation, used in gatherings of all sizes (including sabbath retreats, family holidays, and personal days off). Putting the powered-off phones inside a container with a lid is helpful.

Releasing Phones

We surrender our phones
to acknowledge that we are not as essential
as we would have ourselves believe.
And to recognize how essential we are
to this moment, this conversation, this process.

We put down our phones
to put down the false belief
that we can be more places than here,
doing more things than this.
And to commit to being fully present, here and now.

We turn off our phones
to turn to each other and to the moment at hand,
with full attention, creativity, and welcome.

May we receive the gifts of full presence and essential
connection.
May God meet us in this moment.
Amen.

(Cell phones are shut down and surrendered.)

Retrieving Phones

We return from this moment, taking with us the gift of being fully
present.
May we return with gratitude and perspective

92

to the tasks before us and the noise around us,
a little more willing to resist the urgency,
and a little more able to receive the quiet gifts of each moment
where God is present alongside us.
Amen.

(Cell phones are reclaimed.)

Source: Kara K. Root, *Receiving This Life* (Fortress, 2023), 62.

Faith in an Uncontrollable God: A Gospel Glimpse

What is the shape of faith in an uncontrollable God? What does it look like to live in receptivity to and trust in uncontrollability, as Cuthbert did? There's a scene in the Gospels where the disciples get a crash course in uncontrollability, reframing their faith. It opens with what the church has come to call the transfiguration (Matt. 17). Jesus brings a few disciples up to a mountaintop for an inexplicable experience that feels like a metaphor itself. Long-dead ancestors of the faith, now living and breathing, are chatting it up in a private conversation with a dazzlingly dressed Jesus, whose face shines like the sun. Peter attempts to take control—to manage and maximize the experience. But he gets mercifully ignored and then loudly interrupted by a proclamation from heaven, echoing Jesus's baptism. The disciples fall to the ground in fear and awe, like the hillside shepherds did on the night of Christ's birth, and surrender to the uncontrollable experience. When they return to the valley, they meet up with other disciples who have just failed to heal a sick child.

While on the mountain, the power of the uncontrollable God cannot be contained in tents of their making; and down in the valley, the power of the uncontrollable God cannot be summoned or commanded by their efforts. On the mountain—the voice from the heavens declares, "This is my son, whom I love;

with him I am well pleased. Listen to him!" In the valley—the voice of a heartbroken father declares, in so many words, "This is my son, whom I love; with him I am well pleased. He is very ill. Please help him!" When the two stories collide, Jesus heals the child, and the disciples wonder why they could not.

Translations through the years have called the child's overpowering condition everything from the diagnosable (and ostensibly controllable or at least treatable)—epilepsy, seizures—to the inexplicable and mysterious—"moonstruck" and "frantike" (ca. 1536). Regardless, it's safe to say that this boy loses control of his body and becomes unable to keep himself from harm. It's terrifying for him and those who love him. The father cannot control his son or control the environment around him to keep his son safe. He is shaken, afraid for his son, and bereft of any hope.

Perhaps there's no modern way to medicalize this language, because in every translation, Jesus casts out the demon and the child is healed—which is to say, whatever had the child under its control vanishes at Jesus's command. The beloved Son heals the beloved son, and the boy is restored to wholeness. But the part of this story we moderns get hung up on is Jesus's answer to the disciples when they ask why *they* couldn't heal the child. "If you have faith the size of a mustard seed, you will say to this mountain, 'Move from here to there,' and it will move" (Matt. 17:20).

"As small as a mustard seed" was a common phrase in that day, meaning the absolute smallest possible amount. We assume the disciples had *less* than even that and therefore needed to *get more* faith—we, of course, see it as a mandate toward growth. They needed to build up their pathetic faith *at least* to the tiny size of a mustard seed. They needed more resources, a stronger, bigger faith. And since that miniature faith can "move mountains," clearly none of us has yet achieved a mustard-seed-sized faith. We tell ourselves that if we had "more" faith

94

or "stronger" faith we could control the uncontrollable. A seed that is no bigger than the period at the end of a sentence becomes a measurement device against which we compare ourselves. We have even less than *that* much faith!? How can we *get* more so we can *do* more? In retelling this story, we emphasize the potential inside a tiny mustard seed—it can grow into a vast tree, as wide as it is tall! Grow your tiny faith bigger so it can do immense things!

But if that's what Jesus was after, he surely could have chosen a better metaphor. He could have used a legit measuring device: "You have a gram of faith but you need a pound." He could have encouraged a strong, sturdy, robust faith like the little pig's house made of stone instead of straw. He could've lyricized their rain-puddle faith becoming a deep well. But he chose instead the figure of speech that calls out the famously smallest, most insignificantly sized item to describe the kind of faith they should have.

So what kind of faith *did* they have at that moment? Maybe instead of mustard-seed faith they had faith like a battering ram or faith like a gill net. Or—to put it into today's imagery—what if the disciples were trying to heal the child with faith like a bulldozer or faith like a vending machine? Perhaps they had faith like a bus driver's megaphone blaring on a kindergarten field trip, a washer agitating during its spin cycle, or a plane coasting at 30,000 feet on autopilot—which is to say, maybe their brand of faith tried to exert control, dominate circumstances, steer the world in the direction they thought it should go—even the direction they knew God wanted it to go. Perhaps instead of living in the trust of receptivity to the God who was meeting them in uncontrollability, they were seeking to manage the moment themselves. Maybe their faith was a faith that sought to *control God* instead of *wait for God*.

Jesus's metaphor for ideal faith is the tiniest, least substantial thing imaginable, barely visible at all. He chooses a *get out of the way and don't make it about you* kind of object. He uses a thing that can't do anything by itself at all. A seed needs soil, sun, and water to be altered and changed. A mustard seed is crushed and used for flavor and spice or buried in the darkness of the earth to break open and grow very slowly into a vast tree able to host birds and to shade animals. None of this can be done on its own volition or by its own strength. It must just be, waiting and ready. That's how Jesus describes faith that participates in God's uncontrollable healing.

We cannot control much of anything. If we think that somehow faith in Jesus Christ gives us more control, we're going to be sorely disappointed. We can't control the mountaintop glimpses of divinity, the big-picture, long-story, wide-vista moments of resonance, and we can't control the valley-deep anguish of sickness, despair, and great suffering, which are moments of resonance themselves. The disciples were reminded that we don't make hope or healing happen. We *instead remain open, ready, waiting, available for* the hope or healing of God to move through us.

God is uncontrollable. It's admittedly frustrating not to be able to operate God like an automobile or an ATM machine. But next to our suffering is where the Son of God comes. Jesus takes all suffering into himself so that nothing can separate us from love and so that we can live already inside God's promise that all will culminate in wholeness and healing for every person and for this whole earth. So we join our voices with all the suffering children and the faithful, heartbroken parents in Scripture and throughout the world who cry, "Lord, have mercy on my child."

Foolproof, airtight, high-speed, robust, polished, shiny faith does us no good. Effective, confident faith, faith that seeks to control outcomes and maximize miracles, offers nothing when death rears up and the monstrous looms. It is the faith that meets us in uncontrollability and suffering—honest, longing faith—that brings us into God's presence and opens us to God's activity.

Our faith is not an outlet mall, a brokerage account, or a CrossFit gym. Our faith is a mustard seed, tiny, barely visible, nothing to brag about, but ready and waiting for the master chef and chief gardener: the world-shaping, mountain-moving, uncontrollable God, who will turn our faith into something God will use to bring healing, hope, and life. We need faith that gets plunged into darkness and broken open. Faith that this part is not the whole story. There's more to come, and even though we can't bring it, we can watch for it and ask for it and be ready for it. We need the kind of faith that lets go— lets go of our need to understand and control God, lets go of our attempts to use God as a means to our desired ends, lets go even of our beloved ones, entrusting them to an uncontrollable God even as we wait together for God's redemption. Because the God who acts will act, sending eagles and angels and the quiet, hilltop cairns of pilgrims gone by to feed us in our need.

Finishing Day 1

As we come down the purple mountains and walk through the woods toward St. Boswells, we are famished. Yet there are no fresh fish dropped from the claws of eagles or warm bread left by angels—just a few smashed granola bars buried in our day packs to keep us going. Even with an accidental mile or two detour, circling the base of one of the Eildons before re-joining our trail, we make it to Newtown St. Boswells earlier than we'd imagined we would. We agree it was a pretty easy walk. Most pilgrims keep going, walking another ten miles to the Harestanes Visitor Centre before stopping for the night in Jedburgh. Our plan is to do that part of the trail tomorrow. We're still jet-lagged and ready to rest, but the pub we'll be staying above is not open yet. Kara stashes the walking stick she's already grown attached to in the bushes while we go inside the local co-op to gather provisions. After shopping, we retrieve the precious stick and plop down right on the curb of the co-op parking lot. Packaged sandwiches and "crisps" taste so good when you've been walking all day.

After dinner the pub still isn't open, so we walk a mile or so to a garden center with a café and post up in a booth with some icy drinks and our journals until we can go back. (Here is where Kara feels it's important to say this 63.5-mile trip is more like 90-something: We put many more miles on our legs than the actual trail did!)

Finally, we check into our quaint and comfy rooms, and we're showered and sleeping soundly within the hour, looking forward to taking on the next day's ten miles.

What we don't know is that there will never again be an easy walk. In many ways, our pilgrimage will really begin on this next leg of our journey. This next stretch will be painful, but it will also join us, in happenstance, with other pilgrims. On this leg we will be transformed from walkers into pilgrims. It's toward the end of tomorrow's grueling leg that we will meet our first trail companions: Banana Split and the Three Maidens.

5

Losing Grip

Pilgrimage, Day 2: Newtown St. Boswells to Harestanes

The first half of St. Cuthbert's Way—the part in Scotland—is in the shadow of abbeys. There are at least four abbey ruins just off the path, though none of them are on the actual trail itself. Often where an abbey rests is where you do too. You walk all day, reach the stopping point, and walk or usually cab to the nearby village to sleep. Those beautiful ancient villages of the Scottish Borderlands are built around abbeys. The contemporary hamlet is still wrapped around the abbey's remains. This is the case with our destination for day 2. We're walking to the Harestanes Visitor Centre. (We giggle at the name and let the puns fuel us for a half mile or so.) Harestanes will be our stopping point.

This morning we picnic along the trail under a bridge—pastries and fruit but no protein or coffee—and we're having a tough time getting going. The relative ease of our first day deceived us. We did seven miles yesterday with no problems and on much less sleep. What's three more miles? We figure ten miles today will be nearly as painless. We're wrong. We make this miscalculation because almost all the ten miles ahead of us are beside the Tweed River. This means they're flat miles, with little climbing. We think those flat miles will be easy, so we add in a detour. After all, yesterday we negotiated the purple mountains with ease! Less than a mile into the walk, Maisy suggests we cross the bridge over the Tweed, leaving St. Cuthbert's Way, and detour to see the Dryburgh Abbey. It's a mile and a quarter to the abbey, meaning we've just made our ten-mile walk into twelve and a half.

Cheerfully traversing a picturesque suspension bridge over the Tweed, we pause to take in the huge William Wallace statue towering above the trees in the distance. We're wide awake, the sun is shining, and we're feeling great. By the end of the day, we'll be dragging hard.

The Dryburgh Abbey played its part in conflict between Scotland and England over a thousand years ago. There are even stories of demonic forces being cast from this abbey. We get to the gates before it opens. Of course. Twice now, our timing and the opening of an abbey are unsynchronized. Today we don't have time to wait; the walk is too long. A groundskeeper kindly lets us in for a quick look and to use the toilet. (We've learned now, like preschoolers, to use a bathroom when it's available, whether necessary or not.) The stop is sufficient enough to justify checking off abbey number two (of four) in our imaginary Borderlands Abbey Punch Card.

We retrace our steps back across the bridge to St. Cuthbert's Way. Kara is gleeful about her "perfect" walking stick and keeps suggesting we find one too and see how helpful it can be. We insist we're fine, and she finally drops the subject. For the rest of the morning and into the early afternoon the miles seem to melt away. Then suddenly the progress seems to seize. A dense fatigue comes over all of us. The closer we get to Harestanes, the farther away it feels. Our muscles are aching; our bodies feel heavy. The last three or four miles are a heartless slog.

"Where Are You Coming From?"

In the midst of this strain we see *them*. We've now walked more than sixteen miles over two days, seeing almost no one. But there they are, fellow pilgrims who we'll come to know as Banana Split and the Three Maidens (for reasons to be made clear shortly), sitting just feet off the trail and resting in the welcoming shade of a tree. We will see them on every leg from this point on.

As we approach, we wave and say hello. All four wave back. One woman says in what sounds like an English accent, "Where are you coming from?"

We walk over to them, and Andy answers, "We're coming from Minneapolis in the States." It becomes instantly clear that he's answered incorrectly. "No, no," the pilgrim corrects us with an eye roll. "Where are you coming from *today*?" This correction is informative and formational. It signals that this is not tourism; this is a pilgrimage. This is not about where you're from or how you've reached this place for your own pleasure. This traveler is uninterested in our lives outside this spiritual walk, and rightly so. The gift of a pilgrim is to be on only the pilgrimage, coming and going from one sleep to the next, with your mind on only the trail.

To be sure, a pilgrimage includes coming from and going to somewhere. But this from and to is measured solely by the path. There is nothing outside the path. On the path we walk and pray—nothing else is needed. Together on this path we have our beings, right here, right now, walking this ground, on this journey. There is nowhere else but this path and the God we meet on it. At least for right now. For the time of this walk. We are walking in the time of this journey together. What is outside this journey is to be released. We must let go so that we can remember that we are alive. We are living creatures in an uncontrollable world, seeking with each weary step a God who is wild.

Being on the path and keeping our minds on the path reminds us that the world is not made for our possession. It is not consumable. Tourists leave home to reach the world, never leaving behind what is. The tourist goes into the world hoping to add to what they have, enhancing their collection with new experiences from their travels. But on a pilgrimage, all is left behind. Ancient pilgrims even gave their last will and testament before they walked. Therefore, where the pilgrim comes from can be measured only from the last sleep. They are on the trail, nowhere else. The pilgrim is a pilgrim; other marks of their identity are secondary, even in a sense abandoned, on the trail. The pilgrim lives as Jesus himself, without a den or a nest (Matt. 8). Jesus is coming, journeying toward us, coming to us from his last stop. Jesus is the incarnate Word tenting in human flesh (John 1) without a place to lay his head, without a mortgage or a planned cruise, because he is not a resident or even a citizen but a pilgrim.

"Where are you coming from?" is a question that asks for testimony, for witness. This question is draped in the eschatological, in the longing for deep transformation. The question "Where are you coming from?" wants to know where you are on this journey into uncontrollability. It wants to know where you are inside this promised future that you, with each step, can join by letting go of your own control. The question wants to know how the walk is meeting you, how you are being reached, even called, right here on this path.

A tourist can look like a pilgrim, but everything is flipped and distorted. The tourist is not reached by the world but instead reaches for the world. The tourist is not called by what is outside themself but follows their own inner call for satisfaction and enjoyment. The tourist, like the pilgrim, leaves home and enters the world, but the tourist does so not to make the path their home, being fully in the now, but to extract pleasures from the places they consume.

For a pilgrim, the world draws near as they attend only to the path. The pilgrim receives gifts. The tourist consumes and ranks each amusement. For the tourist, ironically, the world withdraws even as the tourist reaches with more and more verve for the pleasures of the world. We are longing to be pilgrims, but it is ever more difficult as late-modern middle-class people to escape the tentacles of tourism.

The Paradox According to Rosa

Hartmut Rosa wants to explore this paradox we've started to lean into above. Rosa wants us to see how the world itself is fickle, but not in a devious way—more so in a beautifully shy way. When we try to control the world—our ambition wanting to grab it tightly because we want to enjoy it, forcefully sucking the marrow from it—it bashfully withdraws from us. The world cannot be related to as a pure object to control. We are intended to relate to the world in a different way. When we try to control the world, even because we think we love the world, Rosa wants us to see that what we receive in return is not connection to the world but the world's sudden disappearance. Ultimately, our points of contact with the world dissolve. Control makes the lush beauty of the world vanish, leaving only a hard, dry shell. In *The Uncontrollability of the World*, Rosa wants us to understand why control appeals to us and to see why even attempting this impossible modern feat of controlling the world sends the world into hiding. We have trumped the hubris of Icarus, seeking to grasp the sun and take control of it. We want the warmth so much that we burn ourselves trying to bottle the world. The more that our reach into the world is molded by control, the more the beauty and wonder of the world, its tangible spiritual depth, slips out of our greasy grip. The fastest way to strip us of our points of connection with the world, and make the world recede from us, is to try and control the world and all our relationships within it.

There is an extremely important warning here for parents and church leaders! We can all be tempted to use the loss of resources and the absence of growth to get a child's or a congregation's attention and move them into the world. For instance, we know of a church consulting organization that says, "We use the grim statistics of lost members and resources to get a congregation or denomination to listen. We tell them that if they don't do something quickly, they'll die. We want to wake them up. Then once we have their ear, we talk to them about what God is doing." We also know a parent who says, "I hate when my kid is just staring at his computer. When I notice that, I tell him that while he's wasting his time there are other kids passing him up. I don't want him stressed; I don't even want him sitting around doing math problems or something. I just want him to stop playing video games all day and enter the world."

Though such reactions are understandable, Rosa believes that these attention-grabbing strategies have ominous consequences. Control won't work. But what's more, such actions and rhetoric are downright cancerous, making the world itself withdraw from us, doing the very *opposite* of what we hoped to do with our attention-grabbing rhetoric.

Such shock strategies might jolt a child or congregation into action, but this approach short-circuits connection. It will never invite people into the world. Because this type of action is cleaved to a desire for growth and control, it will cause the world—and its free invitation to just be—to disappear. The parent and the consultant use such rhetoric because they want the child or congregation to reach for the world. They want them to feel a sense of vim and zest. They want them motivated and alive. But motivation engendered by alarming warnings to grow and get control *or else* will only lead people to grasp for the world in a way that will make it disappear. The more we want to control the world—make it all *visible, reachable, manageable*, and *useful*—the more the world withdraws. We end up connecting to the world as points of aggression because the world fickly hides itself from us. We work in opposition to our own aim. Our desperate grabbing for control leads us to manifest the very thing we fear: an isolating, unmoved, and disconnected feeling of discontent.

Forcing the Uncontrollable: The Tourist Trap

This paradox of wanting the world so badly that we seek to control it while inadvertently causing the world to retreat from us is the conundrum of the tourist (we know from experience!). Late-modern people rarely admit it, and it would never appear on a vacation club's Instagram feed, but the tourist is trapped in the tragic. The tourist rushes out, believing that there is something important and full for them in the world. As good parents and church leaders, we rush our children and congregations out into the world, wanting them to reach deep into the world, to experience life as full and good. Never more than on vacation is life packaged as good and full. We seek control for the sake of growth so that we have the resources to reach further into the world. Yet, as the tourist reveals, this reach for control gives us only a stale world full of disappointments. In longing for resonance—the awakeness of being reached by something outside ourselves, being moved and transformed by something uncontrollable—we try to force the world to speak to us, to manipulate the unmanageable moment into occurring. The tourist is the perfect illustration of the modern effort to produce an uncontrollable experience through the means of control.

105

The tourist's paradoxical longing for the world that leads the world to withdraw is exactly what writer and director Mike White explores in his critically acclaimed HBO series *The White Lotus*. Mike White is a master at presenting both the longings and the spiritual disease of this paradox. The series is set in a high-end resort chain that caters to super-rich tourists. Season 1 is set at the White Lotus Resort in Maui, season 2 at the White Lotus Resort in Sicily, and season 3 in Thailand. The series poignantly explores the tragic conundrums that come to those who have all the resources to reach the world and yet find themselves bankrupt. Particularly for these kinds of wealthy tourists, bathed in the modern obsession with control as the ultimate tool for engaging the world and finding much success in using it, the world should be within complete reach. Their vast amounts of money should prevent any obstacle that would keep them from accessing the depths of the world.

Yet again and again, as White shows, the world withdraws from those who seek to (and even presume they can) control it. These rich tourists are in a beautiful location, the world at their fingertips, and yet they're miserably dissatisfied. With the world disappointingly withdrawing, things inevitably get aggressive. Each season's plot begins with a flash-forward to a dead body. We see the dead body in the first scene, appearing as a shock that shatters the gloss of the tourist illusions. In season 1, we look on from the airport gate as a body in a box is placed in the cargo haul of a plane. Season 3 opens with a gunshot and a body brushing up against a fleeing guest who is wading through a resort lagoon. Season 2 starts with the jarring juxtaposition of a dead body floating next to a vacationing body in blue Mediterranean waters. The dead body brushes the leg of the bikinied tourist as she swims in the waters off the White Lotus's gorgeous, exclusive beach. The rest of the season's episodes fill the viewer in on how a dead body could possibly become part of this dream vacation—it was not in the brochure! Mike White's point is, how *couldn't* it be? Inside the disappointments of the withdrawing world, of having all the means to get anything they want but not being able to get that elusive taste of resonance, the controlling demands of the wealthy tourists ramp up, becoming more desperate. The points of aggression get more intense. Each dead body ultimately represents a dead, withdrawn world. Dead bodies (at least metaphorically) and souls in malaise (completely and actually) are the result of an all-out pursuit by the tourists to force the world to respond to their cravings.

In each season, Mike White focuses on a different device used by these tourists to gain control: money, sex, and religion. In season 1, money is the device used to reach and control the world. More money is assumed to mean more access to the treasures of the world. But in the end it produces the opposite, driving each character only deeper into themselves instead of out into the world to meet the world. It leads them to obsess over what they have in comparison to others. One honeymooner is convinced he's being cheated and not given the best room in the resort, which he paid for. He can't let this go, because he assumes that this room will allow him to experience something *more* of the world. He wants his honeymoon to be perfect, so he seeks to control every element. Yet striving to make it come near instead causes the world (and his bride) to withdraw. The use of more money to make the world come close only moves the possibility of resonant encounter with the world further out of reach.

This happens to almost all the characters in season 1. Only the teenage son of one family finds himself connected to the world. This odd boy finds his way through the gloss of tourism to actually be present in a place and available to hear the call of the world. The rest of the characters can't hear this call because of their noisy obsession with money. They are preoccupied with money, but not just for money's sake. Money is assumed to be *the* resource that gives them access to the inaccessible world. But money is a devious god. It might promise you the world, but in the end it will take all your attention, keeping you from ever really being in that promised world. The boy finds connection when he's pushed out of the resort, forced by his sister to sleep on the beach. Only then does the world come to life and call him to join it. Some locals call to him to jump on an outrigger and join them in giving up control and sharing the collective action of the row.

In season 2, Mike White probes deeper. If the best device to force the world to reach for us is not money, as revealed in season 1, then maybe it's sex. Each character in season 2 reaches for the world by using sex as a device of control. Of course, money still plays a part—we're still at the White Lotus Resort—but sex is now assumed to be what will give them the transcendent feeling of being reached, moved, and somehow changed. Yet sex, too, takes these characters nowhere. When sex is used as a device for control, its pleasures turn cold and insipid. The world withdraws, and resonance remains ungraspable. As a means of control (even the mutual control of individual pleasure), sex becomes hollow and damaging. The characters use sex not to express intimacy and experience connection but as an instrument to make the world come near—to manufacture an experience of resonance—turning the participant human beings into instruments, merely means to an individually managed end. This control-oriented and consumer-driven sex brings only alienation and confusion. Season 3 repeats the exploration, layering religion onto money and sex as mechanisms of grasping for meaning and reaching for transcendence.

Each season starts and ends where all vacations start and end: in transit. They begin with the characters boating to the resort. The scene glows with expectation; the world seems open and possible. But the season ends with the characters waiting in an airport. There is nothing enchanting or inviting about it; the world is withdrawn. Worse, nothing has changed even after a glamorous vacation. There is no transformation, no joy of having been encountered.

If we're honest, most of us don't want our vacations to transform us. We want them to give us a break and bolster our energy so we can get back to chasing growth. Likewise, the main characters in the show return to where they started. They went on vacation to reach the world, but the world withdrew, and they remain closed and alone. They wanted to, but did not, hear the world's call, not even at the most beautiful, luxurious places, not even with powerful tools at their disposal. Instead, they've seen its cold, lifeless corpse. With all this effort and spent resources, the tourists are no more alive than when they started. Worse, they are stuck in the same place, back where they began, actually worse for the wear. Vacation is, at its best, a temporary reprieve. These characters have a ridiculous abundance of resources and access to reach the world, and yet they leave their vacation feeling more alienated from the world than called by it.

Tourism is dangerous business. If this is how we parent or pastor, we cut our children and our congregations off from the world's invitations to deep resonance and we provide access only to a stale world full of disappointment.

Loosening the Grip of Control

Our journey brings us to a T in the path. The sign in front of us has two arrows: We can go left to continue on St. Cuthbert's Way or turn right to Harestanes Visitor Centre, just a half mile away. We stop dead and drop our packs for a moment. There may be some tears. This last half mile feels impossible. But we muster the last dregs of energy and push on. Utterly depleted, we arrive at a yard filled with picnic tables near a small building with a refreshment window. We buy some drinks, collapse on the benches, and phone our ride.

A few minutes later, the group of pilgrims we'd encountered earlier in the day arrives at Harestanes. They approach us, carrying an American twenty-dollar bill, saying they'd discovered it "freshly laid" on the trail and assumed it was ours. (Yep, one of the kids dropped it.) We had joked earlier in the day, on seeing them from a distance, that they were a band of robbers roaming the trail for unsuspecting travelers, a point of aggression lying in wait. They've just proved the opposite. While the tourist is on guard, intent on not being cheated and looking to get what they can, the pilgrim is open to the possibilities for connection, watching for encounter, seeking opportunities to share the journey. Our carelessness precipitated their kindness. Once again, we learn.

Our super-friendly cabbie, Scott O'Brien of Thistle Cabs, fetches us and brings us right to the doorstep of Allerton House, our next bed and breakfast. It's a charming old mansion converted to an inn. We leave our dirty hiking shoes and Kara's perfect walking stick in the front entry and make our way to our rooms. At every stop, we're relieved to separate from each other. The kids burrow away in their room and we go hide in ours (seeking Cuthbert's solitude from one another). We rest a bit; some of us shower (others inexplicably choose not to). An hour later we meet up to make our way back down the hill into Jedburgh.

Jedburgh is a beautiful little Scottish town. The towering ruins of its abbey stand majestically at its center. The village is still sleepy, not yet fully awake from its COVID shutdown slumber. But there is a pub open and serving pilgrims. And enjoying their dinner at a table in the corner are our fellow pilgrims! The ponytailed man and three women of the shady rock and the twenty-dollar bill! We greet them for the third time today as we find our table on the other side of the room. We're the only two parties in this small pub tonight.

As we peruse the menu, Kara finds herself overfunctioning. *I keep suggesting food options and inquiring persistently on everyone's well-being. "How are your feet? Have you had enough water today? What do you feel like eating?" I feel ungrounded, grabbing for control. I wonder, am I scrambling for equilibrium or reaching for connection? In either case, it seems to be undermining both goals. With fully functioning teenagers who have been ordering for themselves for years and who know when to take showers (or at least are able to choose whether or not to), it feels like my persistent comments are more alienating than connecting. They're clearly annoyed with my extreme attentiveness!*

I feel a nudging invitation arise. I wonder if I can do this differently. Tomorrow I will try to say nothing. I won't tell them what I'm doing or ask them what they are thinking. When I feel the urge to verbalize directions or suggestions, I will just hold it tenderly until it passes. It will be an interesting experiment. The ground is being paved for what is to come.

Something about a big, juicy, red-meat patty seems to hit the spot after a long day of walking. We're just biting into our burgers when the pilgrim with the ponytail swivels in his seat and leans toward the center of the room. Lifting his brimming bowl, he boisterously calls out to us, "The banana splits are amazing!" The kids giggle. Thus, this group of pilgrims is christened in our family lexicon Banana Split and the Three Maidens. Nicknaming is immature, but it's what we do. (Too much *Seinfeld* corrupted our developing young adult brains back in the '90s.) As pilgrims, we gratefully receive the gift and accept Banana Split's hearty recommendation. Delicious.

The Consequences of Control

There are two Greek words used in Scripture that are translated as "life." The first is *bios*, as in biology, the functional act of breathing lungs and beating heart, being alive. The second word for "life" is *zōē*, meaning essence, vibrancy, fullness of life, being alive. Other creatures have *zōē* by having *bios*: A bird is fully alive and fully a bird by being a living, breathing bird. Birds don't think about their birdness: they just inhabit their

111

lives and are naturally fully *bird*. Humans, though, can have *bios* without *zōē*. We can be functionally alive but detached from our living, not fully inhabiting our own being in the world. We can be human without our humanity.

What any parent or church leader wants for their children or the people in their congregation is for them to be fully alive. We want our children or congregation to feel called by something good and full (by the wild, living God) that will draw them into *zōē*, into the fullness of life. We articulate diluted versions of this transformational fullness of life when we say we want our kids to be "happy." What we really mean—we think—is that we want them to *live*. Not just exist (*bios*, breathing) but really *live*, being reached by and reaching into the world. We want them to find points of connection with the world, others, and God.

But because we want this so badly, we have a hard time accepting that this being fully alive *cannot* happen through control. As with tourism, the more we try to control the world and make it reachable for our children or our congregations, the more the world withdraws. When we assume control is the answer, we're tempted to objectify the world, making all our relationships in and with the world into instruments to be used to gain more control. We come to think that the best parent or church leader controls the world for their people. This causes the relationships we have with our children or those in our congregations to become instrumentalized. We've made our life together about resources and growth more than about persons encountered.

Obviously, this produces the opposite of what we want. This drive for control through instrumentalization creates alienation. Alienation is the negation of belonging. Even though we already fully belong—to God, to all others, to our body, to this world—we feel cut off and isolated from others, ourselves, our activities, our experiences. The more we prioritize control, the more we feel alienated from the personhood of our children, our congregants, and even ourselves. This makes us very modern. Modernity wants so badly to embrace the world that it creates systems of action that produce the opposite of what it desires, systems that instead manufacture layers of alienation. Rosa points out that this contradiction embedded in modernity has been recognized by many great thinkers of the modern age. In their own way and with their own emphases, Max Weber, Georg Simmel, Émile Durkheim, Karl Marx, Hannah Arendt, and Theodor Adorno all describe a deep alienation produced by these systems and pursuits of control.

The *last* thing we want for our children or for our congregations is alienation. But that is just what happens when control shapes our actions. What we want is connection to God and one another. But when we attempt to control the world, we experience its opposite: a deep and dull alienation. Connection brings life; human beings who are connected to God and one another are fully alive, experiencing *zōē*. But our systems of control work against our intentions, producing disconnected, lifeless living.

Journaling and Conversation Prompt

Present Period Journaling

In retrospect, we understand our own stories and make sense of our lives as having moved through different periods. The meaning we make is shaped by the particular experiences, insights, and relationships that characterize these different periods of our lives.

You may choose to respond to one, two, or all three of the questions below. Pause to consider your life right now. Without censoring or proofreading, simply write what comes to you:

1. What period of life am I living in?
   » What are the perimeters and characteristics of my present period?

113

» When did it begin—is there an event or marker that started this period?

» What are the themes? Reoccurring ideas or experiences?

» Who are the key people for me in this time?

» What are the bodily, physical realities that characterize this period (e.g., illness, movement, sleep)?

» Is there a texture, color, or tone to this time in my life, or an image or metaphor that feels descriptive and accurate?

» What else feels important about this period?

For group conversation: invite people to reflect, even jot notes, on the above. Give them ten minutes (or longer if necessary). Then invite people to share their response. Let each person share without interruption—you might even use a timer if helpful. You may wish to pause after each person shares and hold silence for a minute. Then invite the group to reflect on what stood out to them from what the person shared.

2. In my life right now, what is most life-giving? What is most life-draining? (The answer might be the same for both.)

For group conversation: without interruption or digression, allow each person the opportunity to fully share their response. After all have responded, reflect together: Are there common themes or shared experiences? Were you touched by something someone shared or how they shared it?

3. Reflect, pray, write, or share: Where do I sense God moving in this time? How is God meeting me in my present period?

» What does prayer look like for me right now?

» Where am I experiencing silence? Soul rest? Inspiration? Challenge?

» How am I experiencing ministry, as a recipient of care and caring for others?

» What is giving me joy? Resonance? When do I feel fully alive or awake?

For group conversation: take turns sharing responses. You may wish to pause after each person shares for a moment of

> silence to receive what they said. Then invite the group to reflect
> on what they heard the person say or something they noticed
> or experienced in the listening.

It often appears that we don't have a choice but to take control—how else would you parent? How would one even lead without control? In some ways, we don't have a choice but to take control. As those giants of social theory remind us, we live inside systems obsessed with control. At a base level, that isn't entirely a bad thing. We couldn't walk St. Cuthbert's Way without partaking in the infrastructure of tourism. We're thankful that the trains are under the control of dependable timetables, for instance. But living in these structures and systems of control makes it even more important that these mechanisms of control don't become the mold for our relationships with our children or our congregations. Welcoming uncontrollability is the only way to truly deal with the alienation that the systems of control produce. When we let go, the world comes near, and we are *alive*.

The Painful Outgrowths of Alienation: Burnout and Depression

We wouldn't likely say it out loud that "I'm concerned that my child is experiencing alienation" or "I have a sneaking suspicion that alienation is spreading throughout our congregation." If we did, we'd be weird. But we often worry and express concern that our children, even relatively young ones, are burned out and depressed. And we're sure a congregation can also burn people out, becoming filled with a sour spirit of despondency.

Burnout and depression are the two clearest symptoms of alienation. Burnout usually comes first. Burnout happens like this: If we assume that the world will speak to us only if we control it, and if that control is won only by the growth

115

of resources, then we can never stop. Never! There is always more needed. We must work harder and harder to win access; we must seek more and more optimization, even of ourselves, to find happiness. Therefore, we must teach our children and congregations to go all out—all the time. They'll fall behind if they don't grind and give 110 percent. (Or is it 1000 percent now? Thirty years ago, 100 percent was the maximum.) We come to believe the lie that our *falling behind* makes the world withdraw. But as the tourists of *The White Lotus* have shown us, that's not true. What makes the world withdraw is the accelerating pursuit of more growth, more reach, and more resources. We need more control just to stay in the same place (keeping the status quo, as we discussed in the previous chapter). This acceleration for the sake of acquiring more is what produces burnout.

Burnout occurs because inside the systems of control, parenting becomes pushing and pulling, and pastoring becomes cajoling and coercing. This approach is problematic because it's so regulatory. But what's more, the calculating control is so endemic and demanding that it can never be stopped. The world withdraws further because, though we are burned out, we keep driving to reach the world in a way that it can never be met. We keep grasping for what can only come to us. We keep racing, never stopping, never just living in and from the place we've last arrived. There is no sabbath, no slow, steady pacing of walking a pilgrimage, no presence in the present. Only the constant, increasing motion of tired people never stopping. This merciless motion creates a society with eight-year-old burnouts and bullying faith leaders. Burnout is the first symptom of alienation. The second follows it.

Depression permeates a society obsessed with control so much that it produces even childhood burnout. Depression is the experience of the world being unreachable, deadened, and mute. All attempts for control have failed, and you don't have the energy to reach for the world. The world has withdrawn so fully that you feel like you don't even have a place within it, and you simply have no energy to go searching for it again. You lack the stamina to carry the weight of control, to try to force life to speak to you again. Depression is the sense that all your efforts to control have—and will continue to—come to nothing. Exhaustion piles upon exhaustion, compounding the sense that the world can never be reached and will remain always and forever withdrawn. Depression is the realization that the one and only tool you have to reach the world can never—no matter how hard you torque it—turn the screw that brings connection. The world is never near enough to speak.

Bede doesn't tell us anything about Cuthbert's inner constitution. Unlike with other saints and exemplars of the faith, we get no sense whether Cuthbert experienced what St. John of the Cross called "the dark night of the soul." But it seems certain that he did, in his own early medieval way. We do know that Martin Luther was prone to both burnout and depression. This, among other things, makes him one of the fathers of the modern era.

Luther called this propensity for burnout and depression his *Anfechtungen*—his temptation. He believed that the anxiety to work harder and do more, which he knew personally, leads only to being alienated from the world, pushing the doer into depression. This pressure to do more and justify oneself was the work of the devil (this assumption of Luther's makes him very different from us moderns). Luther repeatedly experienced *Anfechtungen*, and so he didn't shame anyone who might also suffer that pressure. He acutely knew burnout and its resulting depression. As a matter of fact, he distrusted anyone who *didn't* have this experience. Luther was suspicious particularly of the theologians and pastors who didn't even acknowledge the temptation as part of a reflection on God and the Christian life or those who claimed never to experience the dark edges of burnout and depression. Fully carrying these burdens, Luther knew there was no way that seeking more control could solve them. He had tried this when he entered the monastery.

The only solution to *Anfechtungen*, Luther believed, is confession and surrender to the God made known in the cross. Only by confession can the temptation for control recede. Confession hands over temptation to the God revealed in the uncontrollable manger and cross and brings relief. The Christian life is a letting go.

Meister Eckhart, before Luther, taught that it is only in letting go of our need for control that we recognize the nearness of God to us, inviting us into God's suffering. We let go not to escape the world but to love the world and to be embraced by it—to find ourselves in the joy of being alive (*zōē*) and free. By suffering the cross, the God of the cross brings the world close, giving us life abundant and overthrowing the weapons of control, both within us and without. In Mark 9 Jesus releases the boy from the grip of his suffering when the disciples, with all their attempts at control, could not. In the cross, God turns the weapons of control into the place where the world comes near in the passive experience of just being together, of finding our lives by losing them in love for the world (John 3; Matt. 16). Through Jesus's death and resurrection, the cross is completely transformed from a point of aggression to a point of salvation, communion, and shared life. The cross becomes the ultimate point of resonance.

6

The Longest Mile

Pilgrimage, Day 3: Harestanes to Morebattle

After sleeping in Jedburgh, we return to Harestanes Visitor Center and get ourselves back on the trail. Today's walk is 9.5 miles. Every day the trail seems to be one to three miles longer than the guidebook indicates. This is hard on the body but even harder on the psyche. Today's walk will conclude at Morebattle. This proves to be a busy part of the trail (a relative term). We meet five or six other pilgrims along the way, and, of course, we again see Banana Split and the Three Maidens.

Maisy's knee was sore yesterday, and when she wakes up it has reached near-crisis state. She'd injured it on an end-of-school long-distance bike trip, and it's acting up now, swollen and tender. We ice it at breakfast, and she puts on a brace. Some ibuprofen seems to help, so we are on our way.

We begin the day on the trail with morning prayer. (This is not as romantic or as orderly as it seems in the telling. It's often begrudging and sometimes perfunctory, but the more often we do it, the easier it gets.) Andy being Andy, we also get in some vigorous theological conversation as we walk. He can't help teaching and ad hoc reflecting on cultural phenomena, and eventually we all join in. Today feels so much easier than yesterday. Starting the day with a big breakfast and some coffee helped enormously. We were worried last night that we might not be able to do this thing, but today we feel strong. It is fun, even. We sing a bit, we see a deer leaping through a wheat field, and we have a lovely picnic in a shady wood that ends with midday prayer.

The beauty is carrying us along. Golden fields of wheat, bright yellow hay being baled by huge machinery and left in tiny stacks or Swiss rolls across fields. Cool, fern-filled forests with tall pines. Flowers growing on vines twisting around rock walls hundreds of years old that stretch in lines like bumpy ribbons across the landscape. We follow long portions of Dere Street today—an ancient Roman highway (first built by occupying Romans in AD 79–81) that once reached all the way to Edinburgh. Without a doubt, Cuthbert walked this path. Today we have long stretches of the feeling of being present—with one another and with the world around us—open to the stories of history and the interconnectedness of it all. The world is speaking and we are listening.

In the morning we meet and stroll a short way with a seminary student and youth pastor couple from Virginia who are walking the trail as part of their two-year-late, pandemic-delayed honeymoon. We forget their names almost immediately, so we start calling them (though not to their faces) the Honeymooners.

The second time we meet up with the Honeymooners, we catch up to them at a shaded resting spot, and Kara spends a few minutes in conversation. Hearing what devoted Episcopalians they are, and how they had intended to bring some walking devotions along but never got to it, she gives them a set of our laminated morning, midday, and evening prayers. Maisy is horrified. She immediately reports Kara's embarrassing religious outburst to Owen and Andy.

We meet another pilgrim today. A ruggedly outfitted German gentleman in his late fifties, walking alone, pack piled high, walking sticks swinging. He asks to "share our shade" under a large, lone tree at the top of a dusty road outside a farm. We discuss the trail ahead—he has a lot of knowledge from the YouTube videos he watched prior to arriving in Scotland. Throughout the day we occasionally pass him as he plods along at a steady pace, rocking his walking sticks, but then we fall behind and he steadily disappears into the distance. He becomes YouTube Backpacker.

We also come across a mother and son who look hardcore. Like YouTube Backpacker, their packs are full and outfitted for camping. The rest of us pilgrims have made arrangements for our bags to be sent ahead each day, with a company that picks up our luggage when we depart and drops it off at our next accommodation before we arrive. This allows us to carry only a small day pack as we walk the Scottish hills. Hardcore and YouTube Backpacker, however, must have close to fifty pounds on their backs. They probably don't think about it this way, but we imagine them as the true ascetics on the trail. Some elements of the medieval Christian tradition assumed that the more suffering one endures on a pilgrimage, the more the walk will mean. The harder the better. Regardless, we can't imagine being able to do this walk with all our baggage.

We make it to our next landmark: Cessford Castle. Situated between farmland and woods, the ruins of this fifteenth-century castle seemingly spring from the ground, silhouetted against the bright, hot sky and visible from every direction. We're happy to see it and rest in its shade. It is awesome, and it also means Morebattle, and the completion of our day's walk, is just over a mile away. From the castle's grounds we can see the paved road leading to the little village. While we're resting, an obvious mother and daughter pair of pilgrims stroll past. Perhaps not cleverly, we christen them Mom and Daughter.

This last mile is pained. Our feet and legs hurt. Once again, the first mile of the day is easy, but the last mile is so hard. Tomorrow's walk will only be about half this distance, but even still the first mile will be a breeze and the last a painful plod.

When we finally reach Morebattle, we walk past a sign from a local guesthouse and pub welcoming pilgrims with a free pint. Kara grumbles about the guesthouse being full and not being able to stay there, and we make our way to a small co-op grocery store. YouTube Backpacker is already there. He's exhausted, his back and shoulders still wearing the sweat-soaked outline of the pack he has removed. Behind the store there is a bench in the shade near a spigot. YouTube Backpacker is sitting on the bench pounding a big cup of coffee and devouring two cheese sandwiches. A package of blueberries rests by his side.

As we make our way out the back door of the store to sit on the opposite bench, we glimpse all the pilgrims we've met so far along the way. Like a sitcom reunion, Mom and Daughter are resting on a bench in the square, then slowly the Honeymooners arrive. We spot Hardcore across the street, and Banana Split and the Three Maidens meander into the scene. Most of them, we discover, are staying at the small hotel off the trail with the free beer for pilgrims. To our shock, Hardcore and YouTube Backpacker, with their full packs, are continuing, adding another six miles today to reach Kirk Yetholm. We couldn't imagine walking another mile with just our day packs, let alone hauling fifty pounds on our backs for six more miles. The sun is low in the sky, and we wonder if it will be dark when they arrive. We can only shake our heads and give much respect to YouTube Backpacker and his cheese sandwich recharge.

We're tired, and we wish badly we were staying with the rest of the pausing pilgrims. Not only would a beer be fantastic, but the thought of sliding right off the trail into rest and from breakfast right back onto the trail the next day is alluring. Kara in particular is disappointed; visions of lingering evening conversation under the night sky with the other pilgrims dance in her head. But when we made our plans, there were no openings at the small hotel. Our accommodations are a twenty-minute cab ride away in Kelso.

Kelso is one of the bigger cities in the region. The city has its appeal. It allows us to complete our Borderlands Abbey Punch Card. Kelso, like Jedburgh and Melrose, is built around an abbey. We arrive in Kelso and find our large, aging, character-riddled hotel, much different from the small, personal, and well-appointed places we've stayed the first two nights. The restaurant has hunting-lodge vibes with cafeteria overtones, like a camp dining center as Maisy notes. But the food is delicious.

We emerge from the dark, florescent-lit building into the bright evening sun and walk around the town square and on to the abbey, built in 1128, which soars up from the center of town. This is the fourth abbey ruins in the Borderlands. We've technically seen all four, but we've managed only a glimpse of three. In Kelso here, it is not possible to amble under the arches and climb around the bases. It was closed to the public for two years during the pandemic with no regular maintenance, so it's now gated off for concern of falling mortar or stone. Once again, we get near but don't go in.

Relationless Relating: Instrumentalization and Optimization

Rosa begins chapter 4 of *The Uncontrollability of the World* with a firecracker of a line. After describing how control has become our modern fetish and detailing its aggressive effect on our points of contact with the world and one another, and God we would add (or our views of God), Rosa says, "Alienation denotes a relation of relationlessness in which subject and world find themselves inwardly unconnected from, indifferent toward, and even hostile to each other."[1] This is very important!

Alienation is what we get when our form of action is shaped by, even *for*, control. Even in our parenting and pastoring, what results is *relationless relating*. This has deeply tragic and acidic consequences especially in parenting and church leadership. Maybe you'd expect a kind of relationless relating with a store clerk or telemarketer (it may at times even be necessary) or perhaps even with your insurance agent or pharmacist. But it's a moral problem—even disastrous and heartbreaking—for our relations with our children or our congregations to become relationless. Something essential is lost. Of course, no one wants this. But this form of relationless relating is inevitable when growth and optimization become the measure of a good parent or the definition of good church leadership, which our late-modern world seems to demand.

Long before Rosa, Austrian-Israeli philosopher Martin Buber called this the difference between *I-Thou* and *I-it* relations. An I-Thou relationship necessarily has two separate persons relating with each other. Both bring something, both are received. An I-it relationship is relationless, being instrumental or transactional in nature. Admittedly, we must have some of these I-it relationships, particularly in a modern world. The shape and speed of the modern world's production, communication, and transportation means that, by necessity, some of our relating will be I-it. This isn't necessarily alienating.

But Rosa believes that when this I-it form of action becomes the overarching shape of most, if not all, of our relationships with the world, the world is no longer allowed to speak and alienation festers. Alienation is prevalent in a society where our muscles for the I-it are overworked and we no longer have the range of motion for the I-Thou. Case in point: we use the logic of the I-it to optimize our relating with our children or our congregations. When even these relationships slide into the I-it, then the habits of I-it have overtaken the I-Thou.

We don't *want* to relate relationlessly with our children or the people in our congregations, but we're so afraid to lose forward momentum that we believe we need to grasp for control. Most parents try to avoid being an authoritarian drill sergeant but nevertheless believe that good parents control their children's schedules, making sure each activity yields resources for growth. Parents need to be out ahead, preparing the road for their children. This is a form of I-it, relationless relating. As soon as playing a sport or an instrument becomes something to parlay into resources—moving from watching our kids experience the joy of movement or music to building up their scholarship apps or rankings—we're optimizing their future and setting them up to interact with others, and even this activity, with relationless relating. Our modern default mode of relating to the world is as consumers, and we inadvertently form our children and our congregations into consumers too.

I-it is the most efficient way to grow resources and influence for future success. We're even told that it's dangerous—even for pastors and church boards—to *not* act by the logic of I-it. After all, it might threaten the church if we became more concerned with friendship and silence than with the church's stable future. It would be dangerous if we spent more time listening and just being than securing what's lacking. The assumption is that without growing members, money, and programs, a church will of course die! And yet it's true that somehow, oddly, a church can actually live (*bios*) even if these members are just numbers and not persons who live, grieve, and die—needing a pastor to shepherd them through loss and life.

Rosa wants us to see that the loss of growth or momentum is *not* our real existential threat, though we're convinced it is. The real danger is when I-it becomes the primary, or only, form of action. When this occurs, we're pushed hard into meeting the world through I-it, relationless relating, producing points of aggression. We burn out from working harder and faster to grow our resources, believing that with enough resources produced by our relationless relating we can achieve true relational connection.

But we never rest enough to actually connect with God, ourselves, the world, or others; there is always more to do to not fall behind. We then become depressed because the more we try to get blood out of that stone, the more impossible it becomes—even with all our honed work, creativity, and attention. We pile on life hack after life hack, only to feel more behind and left out. We become anxious because we're told that the only way to overcome the threat or actuality of relationlessness and find happiness is to control every part of everything. To avoid loss you must *prepare*. More resources promises more happiness for us and our children. Our discontent is engendered by our inevitable failure to produce the outcomes we want through our own control.

Control is native to the I-it but not the I-Thou. The I-it promises (sometimes deviously) the growth of resources. If good parenting or good church leadership fundamentally produces such growth, then the I-it relationless relating will always overtake the I-Thou relational relating. The I-Thou cannot promise the growth of resources because the I-Thou seeks uncontrollable encounters of responsiveness. The I-Thou demands that we stop to listen and truly hear, to see and be seen, to speak from the heart and allow others to speak to us, to meet and be met, to really be encountered. Without uncontrollability, we can never truly be encountered by other people or beauty or wonder or the deep stirring of questions or engagement with the world. No profound points of connection can happen without uncontrollability.

Our family is on a pilgrimage, seeking to step out of I-it relating, out of the relentless pursuit of growth, out of the constant need for control. The irony is that in order to do so, we've invested enormous amounts of preparation and exerted a rigid sense of control. Now that the plans have been set, we're trying to let go and simply be here now. We're trying to be in the moment we are in with the people we are with. It does not feel easy. And it's about to feel impossible.

Be Here Now—A Prayer for Presence

Be here now, O my soul.
Be here now, O my God.
May I be.

Just as I am without pretense or fear.
May I be here.

No other place my mind wants to take me.
Not work or the worries of family or friends,
not what I have to do or where I need to go.
Just here. Right here.

No other time my mind wants to take me.
Not past for regrets or nostalgia,
and not future, for worry or planning or dreaming.
Just now. Right now.

I trust you with this world and all those in it.
(Lift up specific prayers.)
Thank you, God.

I trust you with those I love and all they are going through.
(Lift up specific prayers.)
Thank you, God.

I trust you with my own soul, all that I carry, and all that I am.
(Lift up specific prayers.)
Thank you, God.

Of all life and being, you are God.
In every place, you are God.
In every moment, you are God.
You are here now, God.
I am here now.
Let it be so.
Amen.

Source: Kara K. Root, *Receiving This Life* (Fortress, 2023), 51.

Regret's Grasp for Control

After meandering around the abbey in Kelso, we walk back to the square and, in the tradition laid out for us by Banana Split, we get ice cream. The day feels satisfying and complete. We head back through the vast and twisting dim hallways of our hotel to our rooms to curl up with Netflix and to rest our barking legs. We're happy to have seen Kelso, but the regret lingers that we are not with the other pilgrims in Morebattle. We keep trying to release it and be present, but that elusive ease keeps getting upended, like the moment an enormous, intimidating, hairy, black spider scurries across our floor and sends Kara googling anxiously before concluding it's harmless and we'll be okay falling asleep here. Darkness settles in and we prepare to go to bed.

Then Kara gets an email from the hotel in Morebattle. They ask if we are still planning to check in. *Check in?* It dawns on us. We've double-booked ourselves! *We could have been there all along!* In all the details and planning, we had circled back one more time, months before, to see if that hotel had any openings, and they did that time. We'd grabbed the rooms but forgotten to change our itinerary.

The flood of disappointment washes over us. We consider packing up and moving, but it's too late. The little hotel in Morebattle is sympathetic but also happy to charge us for our unused night. Regret engulfs us both. Kara regrets the missed opportunity to be in the one hotel she'd been told not to miss. Andy regrets the money wasted paying for empty, unused rooms. We start to feel worse and worse about the room we are in. (*Isn't it laid out so weirdly? The big cupboard right up against the side of the bed? The room in Morebattle is probably perfectly feng shui. This double bed feels way too small! Wasn't the one in Morebattle a king size?*) The gratitude—for the shower and the rest, the tasty meal, the visit to the abbey, the cool evening, the sunset-lit ice cream—all gets diluted by the ocean of regret. We're now thrust into the diabolical grip of what could have been. This makes us wish for the impossible: that somehow we could control *time*. Isn't there some way we could just go back and not make this mistake? If only we had double-checked and reviewed our plans again! Then maybe things would be better and our resources would not be wasted! (It's easy to see how anxiety can join burnout and depression as prominent struggles in late modernity.)

We sleep poorly and wake up grumpy and tense to an adding-insult-to-injury email alerting us to three bounced checks. While preparing to depart, we had forgotten to transfer money into that account. We're so deep in a hole of regret and disappointment that it demands a herculean amount of effort not to lose it with each other. Andy takes a solo walk. Kara vents in her journal. The kids stay out of our way.

The illusions of control are so poignant for us moderns that we find ourselves even trying to play with time, wondering if there is an undo button, as with our text and email software. Andy grew up playing hockey. He was a goalie all through college. (This was before the position changed; back in the '90s you wanted a smaller, quick guy in goal. Now you want a monster who's over 6′4″.) The best goalies—whether 5′9″ or 6′4″—need to learn to have a short memory. Goalie coaches help young goalies into this mentality by saying, "That puck is already in the back of the net"—meaning that there is no reason, particularly in the middle of the game, to relive and replay what is already past. It's over. That puck is in the back of the net, and there is nothing you can do to control that. You now need to forget about it so you can be present and concentrate on the next shot. Andy's hockey career ended because he was too short and too prone to review and audit what could no longer be controlled. He tried too much to control the uncontrollable. The practice of being a pilgrim confronts our urge to control the uncontrollable. We must stay on the path and be where our body is. With the puck already in the back of the net, Andy works to let it go and live in the time he's now in.

After breakfast in the same dark corner of the large, charmless hotel restaurant, we call a taxi and pay to ride back to Morebattle, with Kara's walking stick awkwardly wedged between the front seats and stabbing the cab ceiling. As if a cruel joke, we're dropped off at the front door of the hotel we paid for but didn't stay in. Getting out of the cab, we see the Honeymooners and Banana Split and the Three Maidens in the yard. They're preparing their bags for pickup. We wave a good morning and hit the trail.

We begin our walk, pausing for morning prayer a couple hundred yards down the pathway alongside a fenced-in field. We start our prayers, but the air smells terrible. We're avoiding eye contact and mumbling the words as we begin sniffing and looking around. Suddenly, Owen points. On the other side of this fence we are standing by, towering easily seven feet high and stretching twenty feet long, is a humongous pile of poop.

So we begin this new day, this next leg of the journey, standing next to a literal dung heap. We all break out laughing. There's eye contact. An internal shift. Regret is loosed, control surrendered, presence ensured by the overpowering odor (we are definitely *here*, where our bodies are!), connection felt in our shared misery and humor, and once again we are opened to resonance. We've arrived here, now, with each other.

We leave the crap behind and press forward.

Relationful Relating: Resonance in Dialogue

Encounters that produce what we might call "relationful relating" demand an uncontrollability shaped like a conversation. Buber saw this long ago. In the best conversations, we listen and respond, never trying to control what the other is saying but attuning to their words and replying accordingly. The worst conversations, which become no conversation at all, are those in which we feel controlled. Our conversation partner shapes, directs, and edits what we are saying, making it a bad conversation, something that couldn't really even be called a conversation. There are few things more frustrating, even infuriating, than to be controlled in a conversation.

To really be spoken to and pulled into a conversation, there must be a *mutuality of uncontrollability*. We must give our conversation partner the freedom to uncontrollably address us. In the I-Thou, both the *I* and the *Thou* must be free to truly be addressed. This real freedom is not cheap. In dialogue, the *I* and the *Thou* give up a freedom-from one another to enter a freedom-for one another. We do this in all true conversations. I surrender my total autonomy, my grip on what happens next, even what I'd like to say, in order to hear and receive the other person. There is sacrifice as much as there is freedom here. In releasing (imagined) independence to embrace actual interdependence, I point my being toward another and become free for connection and mutuality.

The freedom promised by the I-it is a freedom only to go all out to win and grow, to control the conversation, to destroy dialogue. The I-Thou, however, asks you to sacrifice that brand of freedom so that you might be truly addressed and

131

encountered by the voice of the other. It asks you not to see *any* point in the world as a point of aggression. The I-Thou of relationful relating is willing to lose the growth of resources and the pursuit of optimization—to empty ourselves of this drive for faster, better, more—for the sake of dialogue and shared life. The I-Thou seeks first a kingdom of relationfulness (Matt. 6). Growth beyond or outside the dialogue of *I* to *Thou* must be secondary or even tertiary. The growth of accumulated resources is auxiliary for anything beyond the basic needs Jesus invites us to pray to the Father about (see the petition of daily bread in the Lord's Prayer in Matt. 6). We are not to have our minds on such accumulated resources ("Why do you worry about clothing?," Matt. 6:28). Rather, our attention should be on the I-Thou form of action as it shapes our relationships with each other, the world, and God. This I-Thou form of action Rosa calls "resonance."

Rosa says, "The basic mode of vibrant human existence consists not in exerting *control* over things but in resonating with them, making them respond to us . . . and responding to them in turn."[2] We can hear the chorus of Buber's I-Thou dialogue in Rosa's movement into resonance. Rosa directly builds off Buber's I-Thou, taking the I-Thou deeper into our late-modern world with its many conundrums. But this leads us to an important question: What is resonance, again? And what does it have to do with parenting and pastoring?

More Than a Feeling

Resonance is neither a metaphor for a feeling nor a psychological, emotional state of mind. Resonance can be neither of these because Rosa is building his description of resonance on the pillars of Buber's I-Thou. Resonance has a major part of its DNA in the philosophy and spirituality of Buber's Judaism. Buber's I-Thou draws from at least four sources: (1) The Hebrew Bible and the God it speaks of. God arrives in the world electing Israel not for the sake of building a great nation but to speak to them, to be their God and for Israel to be God's people, to be in relationful relation with people. Though completely other and inherently *free from* others, God chooses to be bound to and *free for* human beings and the world. The God of Israel is not a nation builder or city dweller as much as one looking for a dialogue partner, bringing salvation to the one to whom God speaks, with whom God relates.

Buber's I-Thou also draws from (2) Hasidic mystical prayers as the way of continuing this I-Thou dialogue with the living God and bringing us into relatedness with all parts of the world. Buber also uses (3) the sermons of the Christian mystic Meister Eckhart (on whom Buber wrote his dissertation) and the way of the pilgrim who lets go in order to encounter the one who speaks into our nothingness, bringing dialogue to where there is only silence. The dialogue begins in the deep silent nothingness of our yearning.

And finally, Buber's I-Thou articulation flows from (4) his own deep loss of the I-Thou. The suffering of being abandoned by his mother at four years old shaped the whole of his life. Buber knew the redemptive power of the I-Thou because from his earliest days he lived without it. He found solace and healing in the loving relationful relating of his grandfather Solomon.

There are certainly emotional and experiential dynamics within each of Buber's four ingredients that contribute to his concept of I-Thou relations. But Buber fixes his attention on what is *outside* the experiencing and feeling self, meeting the self with an otherness that invites and welcomes the self into a communion not made solely by the self. Emotions and experiences are essential, but they cannot be understood outside distinct points of encounter. Experience is never really experience without a point of contact, a place of encounter. When these points of contact with the world are relationless, they become points of aggression (shaped by a heavy I-it), like with the man who threw himself on the wall to avoid the supposedly hostile driver. Or these points of contact with the world can be bound in the I-Thou and thus be points of resonance. Drawing from his Judaism, Buber says that the I-Thou is the better, holier way to be. This is the right (righteous) way to act. The law given by God for righteousness is not a relationless I-it mandate but a guidebook for relationful relating, *not* for the purpose of control but for connection and wholeness.

In Christianity, Jesus's mission is to correct this misunderstanding through his own person, encountering persons, confronting the way that the law had slid into an I-it relationship (Mark 2:27). Rather, the law is an eternal gift, meant to shape God's people so we can relate to the world rightly (righteously) as I-Thou, with relations of relatedness instead of relationless relating. In other words, we're meant to live out our belonging to God and each other, instead of living as though we don't belong to God or each other. Resonance is not a metaphor or a feeling—it can best be understood as relationful conversation.

Points of Contact: Distinction and Union

Rosa reminds us that resonance is an acoustic description. Resonance is like joining a song, like finding ourselves singing with others, pulled in, being addressed and addressing another. To resonate is to join a conversation with our own voice, our own mind and being, and yet find our voice in harmony and synchrony with others. Resonance finds union or communion while never losing our own unique voice inside the relation. To resonate is to be unquestionably in relationful relating. We can't resonate without keeping the distinctiveness of the *I* and the *Thou*, and yet even in this necessary distinctiveness we are nevertheless deeply connected.

Resonance has a generative paradox not unlike what the Christian tradition claims of the sacraments. At the heart of the sacraments is what might be called a dialogical union of indissoluble difference, which is to say the elements remain what they are but also become something more. The sharing of the bread and wine and the pouring of the waters of baptism resonate with Jesus's real presence so deeply that though these elements remain bread, wine, and water, they become the means of a direct point of contact with the living Christ. The sacraments bring forth a resonance of encounter with Jesus's real presence at the vertical (between us and God), horizontal (between us and each other), and material (concretely real) levels of our existence. The bread, wine, and water host a true relatedness with Christ himself. A mystical resonance occurs between the sacramental elements and the resurrected life of Jesus Christ.

Witnessing the sacraments as tangible points of divine and human encounter helps us recognize that resonance is much more than a feeling or psychological state. Just as the sacraments are not just feelings or metaphors (at least for many Christians), neither is resonance. Resonance is a point of contact that draws us into connections of encounter. Resonance is shaped as a dialogue. It can be joyful, as when Buber prays with his grandfather Solomon. Or it can be sorrowful, even filled with suffering, as when Buber grapples with the pain of his mother's abandonment. In both, Buber is connected to the world, encountering others as *I* to *Thou*, resonating with others. Our deepest conversations, those that move us into relationful relating, can be light and easy, fun and joyful. But most often these resonant conversations revolve around confessions of suffering and loss. The sacraments do this too. At the table we remember Jesus's crucifixion, confessing how we've sought the I-it over the I-Thou (Matt. 5:23–24). These moments of confession draw us into the possibility of resonance because we find our brokenness and longings held here in this sacrament. We find ourselves in relation, resonating with one another, in and through our suffering, limits, and needs. At the table we encounter a ministering God who relates to us for the sake of being with us and for us.

What could be more central to parenting or leading in churches than to enter such resonant conversations (with or without words)? The very point of both parenting and pastoring is relationful relating, encountering one another not for the sake of growing resources or moving forward but for resonance. The conversation is not dependent on cognitive capacity or conversational ability. Being truly with and for each other is enough. The dialogue of *I* to *Thou* is the very point. Resonance that connects us overcomes alienation. This can't be missed. Resonance is an action, a connection of I-Thou. Buber believes that the I-Thou heals. It heals not in a functional psychological way, giving us life hacks to cope, but in a sacramental way, bringing us to the deepest level of spirit with communion and life. The resonance of I-Thou can even heal the shattered heart of a boy who is plunged into alienation because of his abandoning mother. Yet so often parenting and church leadership shift away from this form of action, instead aiming to control for the sake of growth. We think parenting and pastoring are coaching for growth, not bearing and conversing for the sake of healing and holding. Let us say it more directly: Parenting and church leadership are for healing and holding, not for growing and optimizing.

Wordless Resonant Experiences: Stopping Our Talking

> Recently Kara took the children of the congregation into the dark sanctuary. After all the squealing, shrieking, and exclaiming about the darkness, she invited them to be still and to notice. They all quieted and then began pointing out the beauty—the shadows on the windows of tree branches lit by the moon, the way the stained glass seemed to glow. Kara told them to look at the wooden ceil-

ing high above them. "That ceiling has been soaking in people's prayers for over eighty years. You are part of this place and those who've gone before you. Your prayers are held here too," she said. Kara invited them to find a place to sit or lie down. The kids settled in, and then this group of six- to nine-year-olds (most of them avid, nonstop talkers) grew silent. Kara said a few more things until one of them piped up from his place on the floor, "Pastor Kara, could you stop talking?"

Instead of seeing the usually squirrelly child's request as a rude attempt for control, Kara recognized it as a sensing of resonance. She accepted the invitation to let go of any agenda or lesson and just be present. For several minutes they all lay there, wrapped in sacred silence. It felt to Kara almost too holy to even breathe.

We do a lot of talking and explaining (the two of us more than most, our kids would argue). But sometimes words are a distraction. What would it be like to create more space for wordless experiences that might open us to resonance?

Our twice-a-year church retreats for all ages include one hour of shared silence. People drape across sofas reading, sit at tables doing puzzles, or lie on the floor coloring. Kids surprisingly relish this hour, and people seem to want to be near one another in this different kind of being with. The silence takes on a presence and invites our presence. (Ending the hour of silence with a gong makes it all the more glorious.)

Making space for silence in worship, or before a family meal, mirrors and invites a kind of abiding with one another that often happens accidentally and opens us to the holy. Andy and Owen wordlessly walking the neighborhood, grandpa and granddaughter sitting silently in the fishing boat, watching a sunset while ocean waves pound the sand, resting in the spent quiet after tears of deep grief are shared. *Stopping our talking* often helps us get out of the way of God, one another, and the resonant moment under the surface just waiting to emerge.

Pilgrimage, Day 4: Morebattle to Town Yetholm

Day 4 started out crappy, but it's getting better. The walk is hard, almost all uphill, but the scenery is breathtaking. We set out in cool mist and fog, but it quickly burns off and becomes another hot, sunny day. We journey along a stone wall for much of the day. At one point a cow stands extremely close to Owen and Andy, and they inch delicately by, trying not to disturb it. Today holds lots of sheep, and a cairn at the top of a hill. The second highest spot of our journey, called Wideopen Hill, marks the midpoint of our pilgrimage.

Today gives Kara a life lesson on moving from I-it to I-Thou. *Maisy and I have fallen into an unsatisfying pattern these past two days, and now we are quarreling about it. Maisy is walking slowly, and she's irritable. She keeps nearly tripping me with her stick but refuses to let me go in front of her because she doesn't want to get left behind. I keep telling her to trust me and just let me go in front of her, but she won't. Now my own stubbornness and frustration is matching hers.*

Then, somehow, we break through with each other. Maisy asks me to wait to a count of ten and let her get out in front with a bit of a gap. "Give me one more chance," she says. So I do, and it works for us both. I get the space I need. Maisy doesn't feel last. The animosity melts away, and we both find ourselves present and open to the day, receiving the moments and enjoying each other.

Andy and Owen are out ahead for much of the morning, and Maisy and I pause to watch a sheepdog herding sheep on a distant hillside. We stop and chat with some friendly sheep crowding the fence right next to our path, baaing loudly, appreciating our loud, parodying responses until our whole interspecies group is caterwauling together in the morning air. We start picking up occasional trash we are finding along the way and fall in and out of easy conversation. When we reach the top of the first hill, Owen is waiting there for us. He silently hands us each a rock to add to the cairn rising up from the center. We all move on together.

The relationless relating in which Maisy and Kara began the day breaks open into a kind of relationful connection that spreads beyond them to embrace and include the world around them. Through mutual uncontrollability, they find each other again. It isn't until each gives the other the freedom to uncontrollably address them that they actually hear and see each other. This opens them up to the music of the world around them, to receive the moment they are in and the great Thou here with them: the baaing sheep, the sheepdog on a distant hillside, the brother silently holding out a rock to invite his sister into the moment. Shifting from control to letting go, Maisy and Kara reenter the conversation with each other and the world around them.

What Exactly Is Resonance, Again? The Four Characteristics Revisited

At their most fundamental level, both parenting and leading a congregation are dialogues. It can't be said too often: Resonance is a state of relating, a form of action. When it shapes parenting and leading, resonance invites us to walk the pilgrim's path of letting go of our attempts to control one another, the world, and ultimately the speaking God of Israel. Until she herself let go of control, Kara couldn't truly invite Maisy into this experience of trust and ease so that the openness to dialogue could possibly start.

Being Affected

As we touched on in chapter 1, Rosa explains that resonance has four characteristics. The first characteristic is *being affected*. All dialogues—with persons or even a landscape—start with a call or appeal. "Something suddenly calls to us, moves us from without, and becomes important to us for its own sake."[3] This call comes from beyond us instead of within; the world speaks to us in some way that touches us. In resonance we find ourselves in conversation, connected. As means of connection, mutual dialogues exist for their own sake, not as instruments to get something else. Simply being addressed moves us. To aim conversations for any end other than connection is to thrust them into I-it, rendering them relationless. We are touched when a dialogue leads us to share in each other's lives and encounter one another, not when we influence or win. An argument with a spouse about who does more housework is much different from hearing a spouse speak of their dreams or fears or longings. The first characteristic in resonance is to be affected, touched, moved by something *outside of you*. It *must* originate from outside of you. In response, you are moved not to *possess* but just to *be with and for* that which addresses you. You can feel this relatedness in your body. When Kara and Maisy let down their guard and their need to win, they were present with each other and felt moved and connected, and they felt the shift within themselves. A pilgrimage is powerful because the whole walk is a conversation with God and the world and those we journey alongside. We discovered the same thing in Owen's dark night of the soul: Getting him walking got us talking. Resonance is felt in the body and expressed through the body. As with the sacraments, the body participates.

Self-Efficacy

The second characteristic of resonance is *self-efficacy*. As in a conversation, once we're addressed, once we recognize (once our body knows) that we're being called into an encounter, we respond. The self has an ability to respond, and it does respond. Something speaks to us and we reply. Something reaches out and we reach back. In this exchange, we sense that we matter, that our person is needed. Yet, this need is not a burden to meet an objective or to win some end but a release to be present, to be free for this encounter. We know that our response is welcomed not for what it achieves but because it completes the connection. We contribute to the dialogue. As church leaders and parents, we ourselves don't do the healing. Instead, the conversation, the connection, opens the space where the Holy Spirit moves with healing. To assume it is *we* who do the healing is to give away the I-Thou and create an I-it, where the child or the congregation's humanity is upheld as an *I*, but we are an *it*, existing for functional purposes. When this happens, the conditions inside us and our relationship with our child or those in our congregation are ripe for alienation. The parent or pastor is not a healer but a conversation partner, in the relationship of being a fellow pilgrim, seeking to hold a stance of receptivity for the Holy Spirit to bring healing and hope. This presence, with and for each other, is where healing happens, because Jesus Christ exists in the connection between us.

Resonance includes a dual awareness that relationful relating is much *more than* you but completely *includes* you. What your child needs is *you*, not even your abilities and skills but just *you*, to be, to join in conversation—whether spoken or wordless. Your child doesn't necessarily need what you can give them but just needs you to *be with* them, to know and speak with them as you journey on the pilgrim's path of life. What your congregation needs is a leader who can join their people as a fellow pilgrim, who is open to being addressed, and who responds not to fix or solve but to be with and for.

Adaptive Transformation

When we find ourselves in dialogue in which we are (1) *affected* and moved into (2) *self-efficacy*, we leave the encounter (3) *transformed*. This transformation might be small: We see something differently, we sense more possibility in the world

141

than we did before. Other times we leave a resonant encounter as a completely different person. Our alienation is overcome, our suffering ministered to, our purpose clarified. Inside this conversation—again, this conversation can be with a person or a sheep-covered hillside—we are met. Life becomes full. Time itself becomes full—not of resources but of connections. And transformation occurs on both sides, not just within us. Something shifts in the fabric of the universe because of this particular resonant encounter. We've tapped into the universal connectedness of all things, and in the being touched and touching of encounter, something within us and outside of us rings with wholeness and shifts toward fullness. Even in a resonant moment in which you behold the breathtaking beauty of a steady river cutting through a deep, lush valley with not a soul in sight but yourself and an eagle screeching overhead—even in that moment, you, the river, the valley, and the eagle all are drawn into transformation. None of you remain the same for having seen or been seen in reverence.

We all want our children and our congregations to be transformed. But too often we think this can happen only by giving them access to resources so they can live their dreams. The shape of resonance claims that what transforms us is not the accumulation of vast resources but moments of connection and aliveness. What the church can offer the world is what families can offer: an actual place of bodies in conversation, souls in relationful relating. Beyond offering spiritual resources, church invites a depth of relating that touches the vertical, horizontal, and material levels of our lives. A congregation comprises persons who are connected and led by the Spirit to be in relationship, in living conversation. A congregation, simply but profoundly, together seeks to commune with the Word of God, who comes to us as the speaking and listening Nazarene. The only thing the church offers the world is a place of relationful relating that stretches all the way into the divine. It just so happens that what transforms us is I-Thou relations.

But let's not be naive. This dialogue of the I-Thou—this action of resonance that has the characteristics of resonance, including (1) being *affected*, (2) *self-efficacy*, or responding, and (3) *transformation*—is not immune from being misused. We are creatures made for dialogue. Buber thought the first book of the Torah was communicating exactly that. But Genesis also tells us that the serpent could speak, calling the creatures of earth, Adam and Eve, into dialogue. This dialogue between the serpent and Adam and Eve came from outside them, affected them, moved them. It called them into self-efficacy, to respond, *to take and eat* (echoing sacramental words). In turn, it radically transformed them. It made them aware that they were naked and now disconnected from the very source of life. It brought division between them and God. It was a dialogue gone bad. The temptation in the garden seems like "resonance" bent toward evil. But it is not, in fact, resonance at all.

Just because the story of the garden had three characteristics of resonance does not make it resonance. What was missing was the fourth characteristic—the one we've been discussing throughout this book—uncontrollability.

Uncontrollability

Any true dialogue, any action that moves into resonance, is (4) *uncontrollable*. Uncontrollability is the ethical and moral heart of resonance. Even in a conversation in which we are trying to persuade a person, we must be willing to accept uncontrollability. We must stay open that perhaps in the counterpoints of the dialogue, *we* will be persuaded to a different view. We may see something we didn't see before. Even in discourse of persuasion, we must stay open to uncontrollability, or we lose the conversation and slide into I-it.

All the serpent's talking, which seems like resonance, is a ploy for control in the end. The drive for control is the sign that those words are aimed at deception. The serpent tempts Adam and Eve to seek control for themselves. Sin enters the world when dialogue is twisted for the sake of manipulation. Sin runs loose in the world when Adam and Eve abandon conversation with God for the temptation to have control (knowledge) like God. Adam and Eve don't want to *do bad things*; that's not how sin enters the world. Adam and Eve want *control*. They want the control of being like God and not having to face the uncontrollability of their own creatureliness, vulnerability, human weakness. (Modernity offers a form of life that is tempted to see creatureliness as a problem that we can innovate ourselves out of if we just do the right exercises, eat the right foods, use the right supplements, and apply the right creams.) Adam and Eve want to be like God, knowing good and evil, controlling their own destinies. They refuse to be dependent on continued conversation with God, desiring instead to take control of their own existence.

The uncontrollability of I-Thou reminds us that relationship is always a gift. In relationful relations, we live the gift of being connected, and we find healing and help. Rosa reminds us, "The uncontrollability of resonance . . . means that it cannot be accumulated, saved, or instrumentally enhanced."[4] Resonance is like manna—it cannot be banked, stored, or turned into a resource. As dialogue, resonance can only be received as a gift.

7

Losing What We Never Had

A New Way to Think
About Parenting and Leadership

On Feet and Shoes

Only six miles today, a theoretically easy day. Still, the final mile is the most painful. We arrive exhausted and famished into Town Yetholm, right to the front door of our hotel across from the town green. It's not even noon. We eat our lunch spread out on the grass and watch the Honeymooners stroll past without noticing us. We finish up and are pleasantly surprised to find that our rooms are ready three hours early. The whole afternoon of rest unfolds before us, wrapped in a feeling of grateful luxury.

We're staying in two quaint, cheery rooms above a small pub. The pub feels like it's right out of a Colin Farrell movie (relax, we know he's Irish and not Scottish). It's just how you'd imagine a Scottish drinking hole in a small village, complete with regulars kneed up to the bar who fall silent when four sweaty Americans walk in. We have little energy to take in the ambience or engage the locals. We want only to lie in our beds with our feet up. Plus, by nightfall we'll get more than we ever wanted of the pub's ambience.

Our feet are killing us. It will be good to have a long break. Kara has been obsessed with our feet and this pilgrimage for over a year. She hunted long and hard to make sure each of us had the right shoes. She bought and returned two pairs before finding the right ones for herself. Every leg of this trail, she's concerned that our shoes do not get too wet. She demands that each of us have an extra pair in case of emergency. (Kara's own letting go as a parent will be stretched when we get to the mudflat crossing to the Holy Island. Kara, Andy, and Maisy will take off our shoes and walk across barefoot, as pilgrims have for centuries. Owen will refuse. He will trudge quickly across the mudflats, ankle deep in water pouring over the tops of his expensive, waterproof hiking shoes and filling them as they squelch in the muddy bottom of the sea. Those shoes will be saturated and stinky for the next two days. The point of aggression, the need to control his choice, will well up in Kara, even as the path has encouraged her to let it go.)

Bede tells us a few memorable stories about Cuthbert's feet and shoes. The first is one of our favorite stories. Cuthbert had made his way back to Lindisfarne. Late one night he snuck out of the monastery. A young monk who didn't know Cuthbert well spotted him, figuring Cuthbert was up to something devious. The ambitious teacher's pet watched from a distance as Cuthbert stripped off his clothes and entered the sea up to his neck. Like Daniel LaRusso in *Karate Kid*, Cuthbert stood in the rolling sea to train his balance. Cuthbert was not after physical coordination, though; he was seeking communion with the Word of the living God. Cuthbert entered the harsh, cold sea to focus his mind and talk with God. Cuthbert stayed in that cold, northern water for the rest of the dark night. Remember,

146

monks were the original athletes, enduring physical feats not for SportsCenter highlights but for rigorous prayer. The difficulty of a physical act was intended to renew the mind.

The young monk, hiding and watching, saw it all. At first light, Cuthbert returned to the land. Falling on his knees in exhaustion, he offered further prayers of thanks. As Cuthbert did, the story goes, otters (or, as contemporary Lindisfarners believe, sea lions) approached the prostrate, praying Cuthbert. The animals began to minister to Cuthbert, warming his toes with their breath and drying his feet and legs with their warm bellies. Cuthbert then blessed the otters, and they went to their morning hunt. The young monk, amazed, returned to tell those in the abbey what he'd witnessed. He then confessed it all to Cuthbert, and Cuthbert blessed the young monk as he did the otters.

Cuthbert's otter foot warmer story is coupled in Bede with a

Cuthbert in the water and later warmed by the sea creatures

story about shoes. After Cuthbert's death, a man was struck with paralysis. The affliction had begun in the man's feet. On the pilgrimage of life this man's feet had given out. The man yearned for healing but also doubted its possibility. The man was in despair and ready to give himself over to his fate. The man's servant consulted the abbot in Lindisfarne. Could anything be done for him? The abbot gave the servant Cuthbert's old shoes. These were the very shoes Cuthbert was buried and exhumed in, when death itself couldn't corrupt his body. The servant returned to the man and placed Cuthbert's shoes on his feet. Immediately the paralysis released him, and the man was healed. Cuthbert's red shoes (better to call them "slippers," the original ruby slippers) are now displayed behind glass in the Durham Cathedral Museum. And for more than one reason, those shoes couldn't be confused for Owen's wet and saltwater putrid black Merrell high-tops.

Cuthbert's healing shoes

The Panic of Uncontrollable Noise

We rouse ourselves from our naps, books, and iPads and convene in the pub below for dinner. Our first fish and chips after a burger-filled week. The kids have decided they've had enough of the two of us for a while, and they let us know they'll be in their room and would prefer not to see us again until morning.

Back in our own room, we adults have a bit of a freakout. Perhaps it's this longer pause that has given us time to feel our fatigue and our kids' annoyance with us. The scent of yesterday's mistakes, left behind in the dung heap, rises back up to haunt us. *There are so many logistic details still to come! What if we double-booked another place?* Then larger questions arrive, hot on their heels. *Why the hell are we doing this anyway? We are only halfway! Our bodies are so sore. Our kids are sick of us. Why are we walking and walking for no reason?* Evidently, too, the town from which we just spent nearly four hours walking, over a massive hill, under scorching sun, is a nine-minute car ride away. People downstairs right now laughing it up over a pint had left their house ten minutes ago, popping in—fresh and clean and not aching all over—for a wee pint. The noise swirls in our heads. The chaos and questions of control scream for some justification of *usefulness*. *What is this all for? After all this, we just go back to work and school and carry on with regular life? Like we didn't just walk for an* ENTIRE WEEK? The anxiety spirals and shouts but finally quiets down as we tuck in for an early bedtime.

But the quaint, restful pub that we knew in the daytime, to our shock, is radically transformed after dark. We can imagine that the young monk who saw Cuthbert leave the abbey might have been wondering if Cuthbert was sneaking off to tip back a few ales with the local fishermen. Tipping back is just what's happening as night falls in Yetholm. In this pub at least, it appears that you need a blaring EDM beat to make the beer go down. We can't believe how loud it is, throbbing through the floor and pounding through our pillows, the steady hum of music punctuated with loud shouts and laughter, raucous cries, and thumping beats.

We're too old and too tired to join the party; we put in earplugs and cover our heads to muffle the noise. But not even that stops the sound. We can feel it in our chests. It's mixed with deep annoyance. This uncontrollable experience is calling out for someone, somewhere to enforce at least some *volume* control. Maybe it's our timid American upper Midwestern-ness, but we just don't feel like we should demand that everything be turned down. Fear of being the ugly American keeps us tossing and turning, curled up tight with frustration. But how we wish for someone to take control of the volume. At 1 a.m., in desperation, Andy finds himself asking the patron saint of the pilgrimage to do something. If Cuthbert had moments of taking control of fires and birds, maybe he'd knock out a fuse in this old pub.

Cuthbert's Control

You notice it right away when you stay in an old pub, or really enter any building in the UK that isn't in the City of London—which is the shiny financial district in the capital. You can see where newer electricity and sprinkler systems have been run in these buildings constructed long before outlets and fire codes. Back in Cuthbert's day (and into the early twentieth century), fire was an ever-present and horrifying danger. That hell was a fiery world of chaos and torture only made sense: Live through a terrible fire and you'd understand. The thought of fire that would never end but would just keep consuming and consuming, the crackling of flames mixed with frantic screams, seemed about as awful as things could get.

Bede tells us that Cuthbert, like us, spent the night on the trail. He found lodging in a small house, but in the wee hours of the morning, hell came. Fire set the house's roof ablaze and moved toward the next. People shot out of bed and raced around to extinguish it. If the fire leaped to just one more roof, the whole village would soon burn to the ground. While others frantically passed buckets to douse the flames and save the village, Cuthbert prostrated himself on the ground, lying at the door of the next house in danger. As he did, he prayed. And as he prayed, the wind shifted, now coming from the west, pushing the flames not toward the next roof but away from it. The village was saved,

Cuthbert extinguishing a fire

150

and the lore of Cuthbert deepened. His prayers controlled the flames, saving the lives and livelihoods of many.

Bede tells us of another occurrence where Cuthbert's prayers saved—this time it was fishermen caught at sea. The current was taking them away from land and safety. But Cuthbert assured them that by a certain date, in a few days, the sea would calm and welcome their voyage. It happened as Cuthbert said. The prayers to control the sea saved their lives.

But our favorite story of Cuthbert's words of control happened in relation to two crows. Cuthbert had left Lindisfarne and gone into seclusion on the island of Farne. To stay on Farne, Cuthbert needed to build a place to sleep, pray, and host the brethren who might come to join him for a time. As Cuthbert was finishing the roof on the austere little guest-house, he noticed that two crows were stealing the straw from his thatch for their nest. Cuthbert scolded them for their deviousness and told them to leave the island and never return.

Cuthbert and the crows

They left. But after three days, one of the crows returned and approached Cuthbert as he was digging in the garden. According to Bede, the crow did everything in its power to communicate its repentance and ask for pardon. Cuthbert forgave the birds. Hours later, they offered Cuthbert a thank-you gift. They dropped at his feet a portion of hog lard.

The story of Cuthbert, and the witness that he is a man of God, is wrapped up in his control of natural elements (currents, storms, and fires) and animals (otters and crows). So, control can't be all bad, can it? Haven't we overstated things?

Don't We Need Some Control?

Our guess is that if you've made it this far into this book with any remaining suspicion, it revolves around your sense that control can have some benefit. Our bet is that you've thought, "Fine, I can see how growth can produce an obsession with control. And, of course, obsessions can be a problem. But particularly with parenting, isn't control necessary? We don't want the inmates running the asylum, do we? That's not good for anyone. Doesn't the very difference between a parent and a child rest in who gets to be in control? Doesn't leadership entail taking some level of control? Can't conversations be planned and scheduled? Don't parents organize and manage the calendar for the sake of living well together, for the hope of conversations happening? When it comes to congregations, aren't leadership, planning, and oversight important?"

We agree. We don't want either of our children in control of our bank account or even our dinner menu (we'd eat chicken fingers and pizza every night). Most children don't want unlimited control either. And leadership *does* matter. We all need to live inside boundaries. True relatedness—the I-Thou—demands boundaries. The *I* must bump up against the boundary of the *Thou*. I cannot enmesh you into myself as though you are me. I am *me* by my not being *you*. Rosa learned from Buber that boundaries don't destroy relationships of resonance but make them possible. We need boundaries to have relationful relationships. Whatever uncontrollability is, it must rest inside boundaries. This is paradoxical and therefore needs some explanation.

Anticipating our discontent and pushback, Rosa spends three chapters of *The Uncontrollability of the World* addressing these concerns, offering five theses on the controllability of things and the uncontrollability of experiences. We'll discuss just two here. Rosa's first thesis: "The inherent uncontrollability of resonance and the fundamental controllability of things do not constitute a contradiction per se."[1] Rosa confronts the false assumption that because resonance is uncontrollable, you can't have a resonant encounter with a *thing*, which is controllable. You can control a thing, such as your great-grandfather's watch. So must resonance be completely anti-material, a kind of Buddhist transcendentalism? No, Rosa argues. Resonance's uncontrollability doesn't mean that the things that we can control, like the music on our phone or our great-grandfather's watch, cannot take us into uncontrollable encounters with life and meaning. Even though we can control them—in the sense of picking them up or turning them on—things can still draw us into resonance. But there remains a demand on how we interact with these things (i.e., a boundary that must be respected).

Works of art in particular can call out to us. An encounter with a book, a song, or a painting can transform us. But for this to happen, we must relate to this thing (that is never *not* a thing) with an openness, with a willingness to hear it speak. It must be something more than our possession. It must, like the watch, reverberate with a history or story. In direct contrast to non-fungible tokens (which are purchased, exclusive digital rights of collection and ownership of a piece of digital art), the point of most art, a beautiful or sentimental object, is *not* to possess it. Its value lies in its ability to draw us in and open us up. Art as pure financial investment violates the boundary of the *thing's* (the painting's or the sculpture's) otherness.

Pastors should know this truth better than most. The things of worship—bread and wine, the altar, table, candles, icons—are objects, things that need to be controlled and stewarded. But such things should never be related to as brute stuff. They demand reverence, a kind of holiness, not because they are idols possessing inherent powers but because they call out to us, though only when kept at a distance and respected for their place in our shared story and God's presence with us in the use of them (particularly in relation to the sacraments). Their purpose, beauty, and story inside a community and a tradition draw us into an openness to hear God speak.

To grapple with the skeptical questions above about the need for control, we'll focus on one more of Rosa's theses about the controllability of things and the uncontrollability of experiences, it being relevant for our explorations of parenting and church leadership. Taking us back to Cuthbert's acts of controlling sea currents, fires, otters, and crows, Rosa says in his second thesis, "Things we can completely control in all four dimensions lose their resonant quality. Resonance thus implies semicontrollability."[2] Remember, the four dimensions of control are to make something *visible, accessible, manageable,* and *useful.* When we try to control things, we try to make what is unseen visible, what is unreachable accessible, what is unruly manageable, and what may not have an inherently applicable function usable. For something to speak to us we need to *not be able to control it* in at least one of these dimensions. Semicontrollability is important, as it is the essential shape of the practice of both parenting and church leadership.

Semicontrollability: It Starts at Home

Rosa begins his explanation of the semicontrollability of things with an illustration of our experience of home. No child loves home more than when they are in their first semester of university or away on an extended trip. Many of us feel the same. Andy's love of travel is equal parts the experience of seeing the world and the feeling of coming home. Home is enlivened and treasured for our having been away from it. As parents of teens, we've witnessed Rosa's explanation of this tragic element of home. We long for home only when it has already been lost. The *absence* of home makes the heart grow fonder for it. When home remains something manageable and useful but not reachable or visible, it tugs at our heart; it speaks to us. Parents are often surprised that when they decide to sell the family house, the grown child who lives far away is outraged. Logically, she should be the least affronted. She no longer lives there; she's made a new home for herself in another state. But being far away makes the thing—the front door, the perimeters of the yard, the creak of the basement stairs, the picture above the toilet, the feel of the carpet in her old room, the smell of the laundry room, the scratch on the kitchen cupboard door—call to her. She'll protest and grieve about selling the house because she is not in that space, able to see, access, use, and manage it. It being uncontrollable moves it from being a house—the backdrop of her interesting life—to a home that pulses with life and calls to her, an anchor in the world made up of things that resonate with relatedness. Homesickness is the taste of resonance made possible only by home's semi-controllability. No one is homesick before they leave. What's achingly missed is the way the things themselves—the sounds, the smell of home cooking, the feeling of a soft comforter—speak of a deep relational connection. A comforter has the potential to be something more than a cover on the bed when it's no longer completely visible, accessible, manageable, and usable. It may become a symbol of love, recalling memories of laughter and tears, being tended while sick, providing a clean, soft, welcoming nest to wrap in and watch TV on Saturdays after Dad has washed it. Semicontrollability—experienced here as the capacity to picture home (or even see photos or videos of it on the parents' Instagram) but not *go* there—creates the uncontrollability needed for resonance.

Someone who returns home recognizes that the experience of home is not controllable. Sometimes we are deeply aware of what home means to us, but most often it's not in the moment of being there. Returning to what we've lost—even if the loss was temporary—allows for heightened awareness, recognition, and gratitude for how this place is more than just a thing; it's a space of spirit, where resonant encounter and relationful relating have happened and will likely happen again. To be clear, nostalgia is not equal to resonance. But nostalgia recognizes that resonance has occurred in relation to this thing, and so it gives honor to the object and nudges us toward openness to being moved in resonance again.

Pilgrimage, Day 5: Kirk Yetholm to Wooler

Our feet are rested but our eyes are heavy as we leave the Yetholm pub. We finally got some sleep but not until the music and mayhem halted in the wee hours of the morn. We crabbily eat breakfast, each of us looking forward to the solace of the trail.

Today will end up being 14.5 miles (with 110 flights of stairs). It's a hot, high walk that is long, slow, beautiful, and hard. Last night, before the ill-fated attempt to sleep, we talked about our pacing and walk. Kara, usually a fast walker, has been holding back with Maisy, whose pace has been slowed by her knee injury. Andy offered to walk with Maisy today to let Kara find her own pace.

Turns out, this arrangement is both more fun for Kara and surprisingly more work. It begins with panic. *Walk my own pace? What is my pace?!*

Today's walk brings self-attunement and self-awareness that feels surprisingly out of practice for Kara. *When I'm not matching my steps to those I love, to the needs of my children, what is* my *pace?* In walking this way, the way becomes clear. This is the moment the lens shifts into place, and Kara realizes the purpose of this pilgrimage. Like a blow, the awareness descends with sparkling clarity: *This whole thing is for letting go of my children.* It's for setting down the mothering she has done most of their lives and letting them find their own pace. (This realization, combined with Andy's deep dive into all things Bede and Cuthbert, plants the seed for this book you are holding.)

Watching Owen's back, far ahead of me—as he walks confidently and straight, carrying his pack, moving with long, purposeful strides, purple heather rising up alongside him, pressing forward unflinchingly—I see my child as an optical illusion. He's my son, and my heart is full seeing him moving forward in the world without hesitation, the rest of us behind him. And then he's obscured by the fog, and when the mist clears and I catch sight of him again, he's a stranger. A tall young man hiking through the Borderlands on a journey all his own.

Suddenly I have a flash of this same view from nearly seventeen years ago.

He is eighteen months old, and we are in the mall on a cold, slushy day in mid-March, to practice walking. He's been walking just fine for a while, but he doesn't know it yet. He will only walk with his tiny, souped-up toddler walker, a puffy yellow plastic contraption with wheels and a handle, which he picks up completely off the ground to turn corners but keeps relying on whenever he moves forward. Today we've left the walker behind. It's just him and me on the polished, stone-speckled floor of the shopping mall, music echoing above, people strolling by. A men's suit store on our left displays mannequins smartly outfitted for prom, a jewelry store sparkles just ahead. Each shop's music spills out its doorway, colliding with the echoey tune from the mall ceiling. I am bending down behind Owen, my hands outstretched in front of him, and he is gripping one of my fingers in each of his tiny fists.

He's marching forward, head up, eyes alert, enthralled by the movement and energy of the place. Suddenly his tiny hands slip from my fingers and he plunges onward. He's walking! A small gasp and he begins to giggle, filled with delight and pride, propelling ahead. People streaming by are greeting him, left and right, and smiling back into his wide open, grinning face, waving hello. He has forgotten me. He's forgotten he needed my hands to hold him up. Because, of course, he did not.

There in the mall, a geyser of emotion surges through me and I stand up, holding my breath, tears streaming. We'd been working toward this—this is what I wanted, absolutely and completely! And yet there is unexpected sorrow and stabbing loss. He is his own independent person in the world, walking where his feet want to take him. I know with sharp clarity that the way I mother him now must change.

Now on this Scottish hillside, I see my son's back once again as he walks away from me. I realize it's the same moment, repeated. I watch his strong, tall form moving forward: He's a stranger, a journeyer, a man. He's my heart, my child, my beloved son, in whom I delight.

My job as a mom is to watch my children walk away from me. Perhaps I am not actually letting them go—maybe I am letting go of something inside myself, my way of parenting. It's time to let my childrens' hands slide off my fingers, which they haven't needed for some time. I don't need to tell them what to do anymore; I need to let them draw on all I've tried to instill in them, then back off and watch them make their own way. I don't need to mediate the world to them; I need to trust they will be encountered by life and respond in their own way. I need to entrust their journey to God and watch it unfold. In the midst of all this, I will need to rediscover my own pace, not just match their pace. They don't need me in that way. They must find their pace, and I must find mine.

For the rest of the pilgrimage, Kara's steps become a prayer, a kind of watchword guiding her path: *Let them go. Let them go. Let them go. O Lord, help me let them go.*

Semicontrollability in Our Encounters with the Uncontrollable

Letting go in parenting or pastoring is not equal to a cold cutoff or a clean break—quite the opposite. Letting go of the need to control our children and congregations (always done out of love) invites us to make a home for them. Letting go allows a boundary to form that will create possibilities for true relations of relatedness. We do not need to mediate the world to our congregations; instead we accompany people in their own journey of openness and discovery. Letting go is to entrust our children or congregations to God as we walk together. The great thirteenth-century Rhineland mystic Meister Eckhart focused most of his wisdom on how letting go connects us to the love of God. Eckhart draws from the pilgrim's way to imagine the whole of the Christian life as letting go to meet God in true relations.

Rosa makes a connection to parenting by discussing home, asserting that "things we can completely control . . . lose their resonant quality" and that "resonance implies semicontrollability." He then continues the discussion by making a point church leaders can relate to: "When we have completely *mastered* something, it no longer has anything to say to us. We are 'done with it.' When people experience a book—*the Bible*, say, or Marx's *Capital*—as a resonant other, this is . . . because they feel that they have not yet fully grasped it, because it continues to provoke, or at times even outrage them."[3]

The Bible is a book and therefore an object, a thing we might try to control by making it entirely visible, reachable, manageable, and useful. When it's presented to people in this way, it becomes completely boring and lifeless, losing its capacity to foster resonant encounters. Instead of the Word of God (I-Thou) speaking what we may not understand or might never fully grasp, it becomes an I-it, a tool in our toolbox of control.

More than a few despots have sought to use the Bible to win control over a community or a whole society. To control the Bible is to do violence to it, and likely with it. To read the Bible without humility—to approach the text as if we can know it entirely and possess its meaning completely—is to lose any possibility of resonant encounter with it.

But the Bible is also the story of the uncontrollable God in relation to human beings over time—it is our story. As Christians we trust that the Holy Spirit speaks through this Word of God differently than in any other book. It is divinely inspired and handed down through the tradition as a uniquely authoritative testimony to God-with-us. To encounter the Bible is to know it as impossible to master. It is always more, beyond, a doorway calling us again and again to relationful relating with a living entity who speaks to us through it. This relating cannot be controlled, only received, engaged. It can, as we spoke of resonance earlier, speak to us and *affect* us, stir a response in us (*self-efficacy*), and *transform* us in an *uncontrollable* experience and outcome.

While Rosa uses semicontrollability in his discussion of the controllability of things and the uncontrollability of experiences, we may also apply the concept to our liturgies, rituals, and practices. All Christian practices faithfully done—particularly contemplative or mystical ones—are semicontrollable. They must have *some* of the elements of controllability, being visible, reachable, manageable, or useful. But if they have all four, they become completely controllable and lose the potential for resonance. In Christian practices, we position ourselves that we might hear God speak in a way that makes us receptive to the uncontrollable encounter with the living God. Cuthbert prays against the fire and the sea current, believing it is not he who controls such things but God who answers Cuthbert's prayers.

Prayer is always semicontrollable. We initiate it, recite it, or read it. We set the shape of it. But as a conversation, a dialogue, prayer is always more than what we can control. Prayer can draw us past our initial words or thoughts into a responsive connection with the living God. Jesus tells his disciples to pray like this: "Our Father in heaven . . . *your* will be done" (Matt. 6:9–10). Jesus teaches his disciples that in prayer we enter into uncontrollability. Prayer is taught and practiced—that's the semicontrollable part—but ultimately prayer is about encounter. Prayer is an act and practice of asking, taking control in our attention and direction. But prayer is never magic. We cannot control God's response or even what may happen within us through the act of praying. If by our prayer we seek to make God or our desired outcome completely visible, reachable, manageable, and useful, we are no longer praying. God is entirely uncontrollable—the Great Uncontrollable Resonance, Love, Source. In prayer we surrender to God's uncontrollable will. It entails letting go. Even by naming our agenda for a situation, we must place the circumstances into God's hands and await God's response. We cannot make what we want to happen, happen. If we are to truly pray, to approach God as *Thou* to our *I* and to have any hope of receiving (or even noticing) what God does do, we must release even our desired outcome.

Praying Without Telling God What to Do

Often a structure can provide a container for prayer that helps us be present to God with all the longing in our hearts but without trying to direct or manage God or without calling our fretting "praying."

One tradition, still practiced in the daily prayers in monastic settings today, goes back to theologian and mystic John Cassian (360–433), who offered a prayer drawn from the Psalms (31:2, 38:22, 40:17, 70:1) that he described as applicable to every human circumstance:

O God, come to my assistance.
O Lord, make haste to help me!

This might also be used to pray for others:

O God, come to their assistance.
O Lord, make haste to help them!

Sometimes the comfort of not having to come up with words but leaning on the words said by others for millennia—joining our voice with all those gone before—can be extremely comforting.

Here is another simple way to pray that acknowledges God's presence and submits to God's agenda. When there is a lot on our hearts or the burdens feel great, and the desire to get God to fix things feels strong, repeating this prayer with our list of people or concerns entrusts them to God's care but also indicates our availability to be used as God desires.

Here now
With you
For _____ (person or concern)

Source: With gratitude to Rev. Kristen Jeide for teaching our congregation how to pray in this way. Cited in Kara K. Root, *Receiving This Life* (Fortress, 2023), 66.

All contemplative practices, as forms of prayer, are semicontrollable ways of placing the body and mind in a shape or stance of openness to the uncontrollable realities of God's action and mercy. A pilgrimage itself is a semicontrollable practice. We take control by planning (so much planning!) our steps and preparing for and then walking those steps. But we are aimed toward the unknown and unknowable. We walk a specific trail—this is controllable. But we walk to be encountered in uncontrollable ways by God's uncontrollable life and grace. The walking is a form of prayer, of positioning ourselves in a state of availability to being met by something beyond ourselves and calibrating our hearts to be ready to respond if and when that happens. Rosa adds, "In my view, this kind [semicontrollable way] of relatedness forms the basis of the practice of prayer, which cannot be understood otherwise. In contrast to what happens in the practices of alchemy or magic, in prayer there is no attempt to manipulate the other side or to engineer a particular result. The aim is rather to feel or sense an accommodating response, the content of which is not predetermined."[4]

Prayer is semicontrollable because it is dialogue. We choose to enter conversation, to be addressed and to address another who is not us. If this is a true dialogue, we will surrender to the uncontrollable and remain open to encounter. We can ensure the *I* shows up to the conversation, and hope the *Thou* does too, but we can't make that happen. Cuthbert is the saint of our pilgrimage because he journeys along the way in prayer. He does miracles, but the miracles are not acts of his own will or control; they are God working through him. In a semicontrollable way, Cuthbert attends and asks, makes himself available, sees the other, and stays attentive to the world—and the uncontrollable Spirit of God acts through him as he pilgrimages on.

Parenting and church leadership are both pilgrimages of prayer, so there are exercises in semicontrollability that seem to open us to the uncontrollable. We set up spaces, places, and times to encounter what cannot be controlled or coerced. Parenting and leading in congregations involve controlling things *enough* to make occasions and possibilities for relationful relating to happen. But we can never *make* them happen. Often we make these occasions by setting boundaries and holding firm to them—not for the sake of control but for the sake of creating containers for encounters with the uncontrollable humanity of one another and the divinity of the living God.

Families have rules, and congregations have norms. These exist not to control the members of the family or congregation but to offer the boundaries for the freedom of encounter to occur. Family trips, coffee dates, long walks, dinners, driveway basketball contests, and projects are semicontrollable practices. If they are completely controllable—if we shut down

163

all avenue for surprise or otherness and lock in the outcome in advance—we cut off room for resonance to occur. To demand that the road trip or the family cooking class be a memory maker, a deeply connecting experience that each person must relish and be grateful for, is to smother any chance of actual encounter. As soon as there is an instrumental purpose—even if that purpose is to achieve closeness and affection—the relationship has become an I-it. We are trying to control how the other people involved are feeling, what they are thinking, and whether they share and are working toward the same underlying goal. This not only violates the I-Thou, the personhood of each participant, but also stamps out any spark of connection or hope for relationful relating.

On top of that, if we're caught up in the relentless drive for growth, for more and better—wanting the relationship to always get closer, the sharing to always be deeper, the experience to top that last time we laughed so hard mini-golfing or sang half the night by the campfire, needing the worship service to be more Spirit-filled with higher attendance and more diversity and growing reputation—we will most certainly be disappointed and our actions will actually work against our aims. People retreat from the instrumentality of such demands, which are often not overtly spoken but certainly implied and felt. They won't necessarily be able to put their finger on why they dread the next family outing or avoid the next church event, just that last time it felt "icky." Pursuing the uncontrollability of a resonant encounter by trying to completely control all factors will only ensure that resonance does *not* occur.

At the same time, someone—the parent or the church leader—needs to take responsibility for setting up these practices or events and making sure they remain neither heavily controlling nor overly chaotic. Both parents and church leaders embody the charge of creating and curating semicontrollable activities and environments that can host I-Thou encounters of resonance. That's the whole *point* of the job, really. We set a table and invite a posture of openness to being met by something beyond what we are capable of producing.

Rosa illustrates this concept with a museum. He says, "A museum . . . is a place where we generally do not pursue any instrumental aims, where we want instead to come into contact with things in a way that is geared not toward escalation or control, but toward unexpected or unpredictable, resonant encounters, where we are inwardly open and ready to be called."[5] What a great way to think about both parenting and church leadership. A museum is a semicontrolled environment that is ordered and organized. No one wants to go to a museum that is cluttered, unlabeled, messy, and chaotic—that's just grandpa's basement. Someone has the responsibility to oversee the museum, making it an environment that respects things and upholds persons. Inside the museum there is an openness to be encountered, to be spoken to—often by fostering an environment that provides for ease, rest, and focus, with benches, wide open space, and the expectation of shared silence, as all those attending are open to encountering beauty or challenge, mystery or wonder.

Families and congregations do the same. They curate experiences and set up spaces as would a museum. The family kitchen has order and rules. Things go in certain places and people take on certain chores so that food may be prepared and shared with one another and people may be nourished bodily and relationally. Dinner happens at a set time, or at least during a range when people know the call will come and stop what they are doing to come to the table. (And if not regularly, in our rushed and overly busy lives, then at least on certain occasions, like holidays, birthdays, or when having someone over.)

The church sanctuary has symbols and patterns. The worship service is filled with thoughtfully crafted experiences that draw from tradition and involve the senses, including movement and stillness, silence and sound: singing, standing, listening, speaking together. The space and experiences created are ordered and organized, requiring control up to a point but not fully, because the boundaries and structure exist for the sake of fostering openness to the uncontrollable, to resonance and encounter.

When there is only chaos and brokenness in the home, with no chance for true encounter, when congregations become environments of confusion, distrust, and disorder, the possibility for human flourishing or transformative connection is quashed. Both rigid control and tumultuous chaos have the same outcomes: burnout, depression, and anxiety.[6] Parents and church leaders provide boundaries or norms not with an eye toward escalation or control but to foster spaces for unexpected aliveness and joy. We can prepare and plan and walk, but life is a pilgrimage with otherness, a journey into mystery and encounter.

Water and Strangers

In the early afternoon, we stumble across Mom and Daughter. We don't talk much; it's clear we've interrupted an argument, or at least met them at a moment of tension. And when we happen upon them, we ourselves have just reached a crisis: We've run out of water.

It's unusually hot in Scotland for late summer. As if a bit ashamed, the locals keep apologizing to us for all the sun and heat. They prefer clouds and sweater weather with misty rain, even in August. That's proper Scotland, they remind us. We're walking 63.5 miles in the sun-soaked Borderlands (and it's important to some of us that you know it was more like 90 miles all told, once you add in the detours and in-town miles). Today, with over six miles still to go on the hot trail, and our water bottles empty, we ask Mom and Daughter if they know where to get water. They're not sure but encourage us to try down the street.

We find ourselves walking into the "office" of a huge estate. A startled young Scottish sheep farmer welcomes us, taking us not to a backyard hose but right into his kitchen to fill our bottles. We walk past the dog kennels and are serenaded by the barking of those magical beasts who can herd hundreds of sheep in minutes. Later, down the trail we watch from a distance as they do just that, racing like a shot from a cannon, rounding up the sheep and herding them through a gate in the fence. We're getting used to sheep and cows as we walk. They are far more frequent traveling companions than any other pilgrims. They're everywhere.

The young man in the kitchen talks a little about sheep and dogs, but more about the trail and what we'll encounter. He gives us some insider knowledge about what to expect and what not to miss on this leg. He even invites us to cut through his farm—that's no small invitation—to a local swimming hole. But we've left our kids waiting back on the road. We enjoy his few minutes of hospitality; they are a blessing. This small, uncontrollable human encounter is nourishing. An interaction between an unplanned guest and host seems to edify us all.

This unscripted happenstance with a young man, near water, connects to Cuthbert—though it would be hard to mistake this young farmer for an angel, or even to imagine that his hospitality was engendered by the possibility that by welcoming us, he himself might be entertaining angels. His gruff response to the dogs' cacophonous barking made that clear. As we walked past the raucous kennels, he barked back at them, "Oh, now, shut the f—— up!" Not very angelic—as far as we know. But his hospitality blesses us, connecting us, even for those few minutes, giving us an experience of relationful relating. Bede tells us that one day Cuthbert saw a young person he didn't know. The young man probably looked a lot like our two kids back on the road, waiting for us to fill the water bottles. Cuthbert raced to the young person, hoping to show him welcome and kindness. Perhaps like this summer, in these same Borderlands, it was hot. Cuthbert, like the young farmer to us, approaches the boy, offering water. Encounters of blessing over water are a staple for the pilgrim.

Cuthbert offers the young person water to drink and wash his hands with. But then Cuthbert kneels and begins to wash the boy's feet. He takes the young man's feet to his own chest and massages them with care. This is something any pilgrim would welcome and be blessed by. Bede tells us that although Cuthbert's hospitality was only for the sake of welcoming a stranger, he nevertheless happened to be washing the feet of an angel.

As we leave the farm, we don't think the foulmouthed young man is an angel, nor are we expecting angelic encounters. But we are blessed by the young sheep farmer's kindness and welcome. Thanks to him we make it back to the road with full water bottles. When we arrive, a cab is pulling away from the curb. Daughter is in the back of the taxi and Mom is now solo on the trail. Mom travels out ahead of us the rest of the day's walk. We wonder what's occurred, what's divided them. We know there is a story there. We can guess it. Not with any specifics, but we know the tensions and battles of control and letting go in parenting. The painful hours of the trail can divide as well as unite.

We follow our sheep farmer's advice and detour to the

Cuthbert and the angel

swimming hole for lunch. We come out of the brush onto a small ravine, with water falling into a deep pool, then bubbling up over rocks and continuing on through the trees. A group of men, with a boy and a dog, are scattered around the boulders and perched on the cliff above, laughing at one who is leaning far out over the water with a long stick in his hand, trying to free a pair of goggles dangling from a branch. There's a lot of free-spirited cursing and good-natured ribbing transpiring in charming Scottish brogue, but the air is a bit charged as well.

Andy is on edge. The locals haven't acknowledged us, and we feel a bit like we're invading their territory. Will this become a point of aggression? We move downstream from them and find a spot to sit. Taking off our shoes, we immerse our hot feet into the icy water. We eat our sandwiches and try to keep to ourselves while surreptitiously observing the group struggling with the goggles. Their dog wanders over to sniff us. He sits down beside Owen and watches him eat, patiently hoping for a crust of his bread.

Maisy and Kara feel obligated to try to swim in the local swimming hole as long as we are here. They plunge in briefly in their clothes, coming up gasping from the cold water. Andy and Owen are eager to move on. We clean up our lunch trash, pull on our socks and shoes, and make our way back up the ravine. Just as we emerge from the brush onto the trail, we hear a roar of satisfaction from the stream below. They must have finally retrieved the goggles.

Life Cycles and Why We Resist This

Rosa moves on from his discussion of the controllability of things, the uncontrollability of experiences, and the importance of semicontrollability to discuss the pitfalls of the pursuit of control. First, he wants us to see the negative consequences on a personal level. Examining different stages of life (birth, childhood and education, life planning [relationships and career], aging and elder care, and dying), Rosa shows the temptation for each of these areas to be overtaken by optimization, making them about control. We're led to believe that if we don't drive for a controlling optimization, then we or those we love will fall behind, and the possibility of living a good life will be unreachable. Rosa shows that this drive toward optimization in every stage of life never connects us to life itself. It only creates many points of aggression. With childbirth classes, birth plans, curated playlists, birthing coaches, and labor doulas on the one end, and advance directives, medical technology, interventions, and death doulas on the other, even birth and death can be overtaken by optimizing control. That's not to say there is anything wrong with using these things—we often choose them because we recognize the importance of these moments and seek a more resonant experience. But, tragically, preplanned resonance is not a thing. The more we try to control variables and manipulate time and space to make resonance happen at these key life events, the less likely it is that we will actually feel something beyond ourselves speaking to us in that moment. Because resonance is uncontrollable, it comes in ways we can't anticipate and meets us in ways we don't expect.

Not to mention that modernity believes life is so controllable that death itself should never be considered. As Rosa says, "Modernity's relationship to illness is one of pure aggression—be gone with it!—and, when we are unable to beat it, we see ourselves as impotent failures."[7] Parents should never be thinking about how they want their children to live so that they might die well. Not even pastors are assumed to be helping people die well or die a Christian death, though this was indeed a major assumption of pastoral practice before modernity. But inside the illusions of control, we delude ourselves into not even considering that we're going to die. We ignore that death is not optional—it's 100 percent coming for 100 percent of us.

We valorize those who, against the brute fact of their impending death, never, ever give up, keeping up that can-do attitude, liquidating their life savings to fly somewhere to try some experimental treatment. Both of our grandmothers, when they reached their midnineties, talked often about wanting to die. They weren't depressed, just finished. They were *done*; and having "run the good race" (2 Tim. 4:7), they were content in the thought that death would come soon—they even craved it. Yet our siblings, and even we at times, refused to hear it. We kept saying things like "No, no, don't talk like that, Grandma!" or "We want you here!" But we couldn't say why—we only knew that we didn't want to think about their death at all. We didn't want to face what we couldn't control. As a result, both women were kept alive beyond their wishes well into their nineties due to late modernity's obsession with controlling every stage of life.

The Four Dark Proclamations (and One Underlying Stance)

After showing how the drive for controlling optimization has crept into every stage of our life, Rosa discusses why this optimization feels so necessary on a societal level, particularly for institutions. The need for dynamic stabilization (the demand that things continue to expand and grow merely to maintain themselves) to make everything limitlessly controllable crashes against the reality that the world itself *is not and never will be* completely controllable. In fact, while demanding that everything be controlled and controllable in order to keep optimizing and growing, we also know that real breakthroughs, true connections, advances in learning and discovery, and experiences of awakened life happen in ways we can't make happen, in moments we didn't control. Our whole society is built on a strained tension between our relentless attempts to assert control and the necessity of accepting uncontrollability. Rosa's point is that even when we recognize that relationful relating—through entering into dialogues with one another, the world, and God—requires uncontrollability, we still feel that if we don't continue to exert as much control as possible, we will meet our demise.

The tension between resisting and needing uncontrollability plays out in ways that can be summarized in four dark proclamations, as well as one underlying assumption, that will sound familiar to most church leaders. These are four statements that we might make (or subconsciously believe) that reveal our resistance to resonance and its uncontrollability.

"We Can't Afford It!"

The first dark proclamation is a firm commitment to optimization: "*We can't afford it!*" Because resonance is uncontrollable—because we don't know what will happen inside a dialogue or conversation—*we can't afford* to build our communities around openness to resonance. If we try to move our congregation or denomination away from optimization and the pursuit of growth, and instead shape our institution around the semicontrollable practices of prayer or relationality, we will run out of money or people. The fear of decline is keeping Protestantism from its very source of life. Rosa says it this way: "Nurses and caretakers who need to account for their actions minute by minute, cannot allow themselves any open-ended interactions with their patients, while universities cannot offer a course of study without making clear how long it takes to complete the program and what skills will be acquired in the process."[8]

Parents' most scarce resource, the one we are most terrified of losing and most desperate about keeping, is time. "I don't have time to hear about your dream last night or sit here cuddling the dog together when we have to get socks and shoes on and get out the door in time for soccer. If we don't listen to these audiobooks in the car while we drive, we will never practice the language you need to get into the school we want for you, to advance your college prospects. We can't afford to spend a day in unstructured activities when there are so many options for enrichment and learning, which other families are participating in, that we are missing out on."

Church leaders whose whole job is to keep the church from closing—to dedicate their time and energy pursuing greater attendance and higher giving—cannot attend to the holy unpredictability of their call. They cannot wait for the activity of the living God and welcome the messy longings of the human spirit as they mingle together. They cannot tend the spaces for transformative encounters to occur. The need for optimization as a form of control keeps us from the deep encounters for which our spirits deeply long. And ironically, the whole articulated purpose of focusing all time and energy on keeping the church open is *so that we can turn our heart to God and share in the ministry of Christ*, but in our striving for control we miss the moments when God is reaching out and Christ stands before us in the face of another. Fear of decline keeps us from what can give us life. "We can't afford it" is a strong commitment to optimization.

"People Would Take Advantage!"

Yet even if we could afford to wait on God or be present to each other through practices of semicontrollability, our institutions holler back what Rosa calls "the logic of bureaucracy and demand for justice"[9]: If we moved in this direction, *people would take advantage.*" For instance, Kara's leadership practice of telling congregants that they should serve out of joy and serve only as long as it gives them joy garners major pushback when she shares that with other leaders. *Those are nice thoughts, but, good grief, if you give people an out like that, they will take advantage and never do anything!* It's better, we assume, to find strategies to optimize commitment than to depend on resonance and the openness to relationful relating.

Endless rules, regulations, stipulations, and perimeters dictate the way our organizations function to guard against risk, loss, and uncontrollable, damaging outcomes. All new good ideas must pass through committee approval and fit under predetermined strictures, lest chaos and undependability reign, or so we assume. In practice, this bureaucracy often serves to squelch any joy or excitement about new ideas or involvement—everything will have to pass through so many hurdles that people are anticipatorily defeated, burned out before they begin. Like the guy on the Instagram reel says, "OK, not to exaggerate, but I feel like I'm already tired tomorrow."[10] (So, see? If we left it up to people's whims, they'd do nothing! Vicious circle.)

"Whose Responsibility Is This?"

We hold to all these rules because if we step outside the bounds or don't follow fixed strategies, our institutions shriek a third dark proclamation: "*Whose responsibility is this?*" If we invite people to serve only out of a sense of calling, who will take responsibility for Sunday school? Instead of questioning whether the community may not be called to a form of education right now that looks like what we think of as Sunday school, we assume that the few will have to do the majority's work, even though the few don't want to. No one imagines that the congregation is no longer called to shape its life around Sunday school. But what if Sunday school no longer offers a space for resonant conversation that can feed the congregation? Kara likes to say, "If we have people serving out of obligation and not out of joy (resonance), then we are withholding roles from others for whom it would bring joy, or we are propping our foot in a door God is trying to close."

This dark proclamation also plays out in what Rosa calls our "demand for transparency and documentation."[11] Should anything go wrong, any accident or unforeseen event occur, we want to know who is responsible, where the policies and practices fell apart, and whom we can blame. When we live as though everything is controllable (even other people's commitment and behavior), we can't accept it when avoidable accidents occur. If our child gets hurt by another student in the classroom, we want to know why there wasn't more supervision. The demand to know who to hold responsible can produce stifling guilt inside a parent or hostile blame toward a co-parent. Terror at being at fault if something bad should occur keeps us building ever more rigid structures and guards against unforeseen risks.

"I Paid for It, I'm Entitled to It"

We can't accept the idea that things happen that we can't control or that allowing for uncontrollability may mean doing less or letting some things go because of the fourth dark proclamation of institutions built on optimization: "*I paid for it, I'm entitled to it.*" Rosa describes this as "commodification and legalism," meaning now we are all consumers.[12] Every object or experience has become a commodity or service that we have some right to control because we have somehow purchased or invested in it.

Because Sunday school is an entitlement that must happen, it becomes the church leader's problem that no one will volunteer to lead it. The conversation will not be allowed to shift into considering alternative practices or experiences that could open the congregation to resonance, because the congregation believes having Sunday school, as they've always had it, is a right, even though no one wants to lead it. The people who in years past already did their optimizing part—teaching Sunday school in 2002—want it to occur even if they don't want to be part of it. They paid to be part of a church that has a Sunday school. Even if they can't participate much, they invested in it and served their time—and now that it's other people's turn to serve, they want Sunday school to keep happening. The church leadership is burdened with figuring out how. (Continuing with the example of Sunday school, the great irony is that many families don't have the capacity for it either. Kids are in school eight hours a day, five days a week, with after-school programs and sports and music lessons, and the last thing these kids or parents really want or need is another lesson or school experience. But they are also stuck in the pressure that it *should* happen. Because who wants to go to a church that doesn't even have Sunday school? How can that be a successful church?)

In families, it begs the question, What exactly are we paying for? Don't we deserve to have the memory-making, family-bonding fun that's implied when we spend exorbitant amounts of money to visit Disney World and Universal Studios? We aren't doing it just to sit buckled into the Minions ride or eat drippy Mickey-shaped ice cream sandwiches. We're investing in something more transcendent than that, and we expect to receive it.

"You Are the Very Destroyer of Things" (Conceptual Control)

Finally, Rosa says, there is one underlying mentality that shapes our approach to the world: "The modern attitude of aggression defines our relationship to the world in every aspect of our existence, down to our 'conceptual control' over the world."[13] We unthinkingly assume everything can be fully grasped and completely understood, and we will aggressively make it so. This underlying stance causes us to overlook the inherent *otherness* of people, things, or experiences. It's so intrinsic to all our modern bureaucracies and daily ways of life that we don't even think about this way of thinking. The problem is that if things are conceptually controllable, they are experientially impossible. In other words, if we perceive things as entirely visible, reachable, manageable, and useful (or even able to be), they become impossible to truly experience. We get preemptively trapped in the I-it of relationless relating instead of being open to the I-Thou of relationful relating. We are already finished before we begin, leaving nothing open or unknown, with no curiosity or mystery. This underlying stance smothers uncontrollability and destroys the possibility of resonance. So driven to optimization and commodification, so primed to relate to the world through aggression, we can't see *uncontrollability* as anything other than something that isn't controllable *yet*. To encapsulate this dynamic, Rosa draws from a Rainer Maria Rilke poem titled "I Am so Afraid of People's Words," which expresses horror at the intellectual certainty with which people speak, a certainty that seems to deaden the world. The poem ends with these lines:

> It's a wonder to me to hear things sing.
> You touch them and they stultify.
> You are the very destroyer of things.[14]

Rosa uses the moon as an example of how conceptual controllability obliterates the possibility of resonance. Marveling at the beauty of the moon and contemplating it as poets, journeyers, and bedtime-window-gazing children have throughout time can be immediately shut down by a list of all we know factually about the moon. Our wonderment at the moon such as what is expressed in literature, sailing songs, and paintings can even be circumvented by reflecting on and unpacking the moon's place in literature, sailing songs, and paintings. The moon becomes an object to be fully grasped instead of a mystery to be encountered in curiosity, beauty, and admiration. By assuming conceptual control over the moon, in a sense, we destroy it.

Kara distinctly remembers an occasion of this happening in her childhood. Riding along in the back seat of the family station wagon, she recalls taking in the gently rolling Midwestern hills and letting her mind wander to all the people her same age in countries all over the world, living at that very moment in utterly other landscapes, houses, neighborhoods, and schools, who traveled here to there in ways other than the family automobile. She imagined her life in any of those places and marveled at how completely different it would be. After soaking in the vastness of this idea for a time, she said aloud to her dad, "Isn't it amazing that I could have been born anywhere, had a completely different life than this one, but I was born here, now?"

Her dad promptly replied, "Impossible. It couldn't happen. You are only you because you are genetically Mom and me. You could only ever be exactly what you are now." The bubble popped, all further conversation and imagination slammed closed. She could not in any way access the transcendent feeling she had been steeped in just seconds earlier.

We moderns relate to what we encounter as if it were fully identifiable, and if not completely controllable then potentially so. Even though we could never reach all the world's mysteries in the far depths of the ocean, the limits of the cosmic expanse, or the most intricate cellular function inside the human body; even though we will always be eluded by the inscrutable uniqueness of every single person we cross paths with in a single day, not to mention those we share homes and lives with; even though our own minds, hearts, and experiences always remain in some ways unknowable even to ourselves, we relate to everything as things purchased, gained, managed, operated, and mastered, or soon to be. This approach causes points of aggression to creep into all our dynamics, cutting us off from the possibility of resonance.

In a congregation, when we approach the sermons, songs, Bible studies, and church picnics as completely controllable entities to be managed and administered, when the church building is just a building, and when the events calendar is a measure of the successful productivity of the financial and time investment of the congregants, we've become "the very destroyer of things."

In families, it's remarkable how the modern age has squashed the capacity to sit in wonder and unknowing, to contemplate mystery together. Any question in our own household—about weather patterns or practices of ancient civilizations or the mystery of the human psyche—has about ten seconds of ponder time before it gets directed to Alexa, who answers it perfunctorily and simplistically, effectively killing it. By shifting to seeing the world as functionally knowable, we have cut ourselves off from the delicious possibilities of what is actually more true: the uncontrollable and deeply unknowable reality of most everything that exists. We've thereby short-circuited the human joy of living in relational encounter with the world around us and the people alongside us. We've inadvertently become "the very destroyer of things."

Congregations and families dedicated to pilgrimage and rest, who remain open to an uncontrollability that fosters experiences of resonance, are thwarted by the fundamental societal approaches to life that we see played out in these four dark proclamations and one underlying stance. As we push against the drive for control, we will continue to bump up against the overt and implied commitment to optimization that often sounds like, "We can't afford it," the logic of bureaucracy and demand for justice that comes out as "People would take advantage of it," the demand for transparency and documentation expressed as "Whose responsibility is this?," the commodification and legalism of "I paid for it, I'm entitled to it," and the underlying problem of conceptual controllability (believing that all things are potentially knowable) that makes us "the very destroyer of things." We cannot escape this adept and aggressive resistance to uncontrollability until we become aware of our participation in it and embrace semicontrollable practices of openness to uncontrollability. In other words, until we learn to pray.

But there are two things that make this very hard to do: desire and monsters. Desire and monsters—or, better, ice cream and demon rings—are just where our pilgrimage leads us in its final days.

MIDDAY PRAYER

In the name of the sending Father,
in the name of the pilgrim Son,
in the name of the wind-like Spirit,
in the name of the Three in One.

CALL TO WORSHIP: PSALM 95:6–7

O come, let us worship and bow down,
let us kneel before the LORD, our Maker!
For he is our God,
and we are the people of his pasture,
and the sheep of his hand.

PSALM READING: PSALM 65:5–8, 12–13

By awesome deeds you answer us with deliverance,
O God of our salvation;
you are the hope of all the ends of the earth
and of the farthest seas.
By your strength you established the mountains;
you are girded with might.
You silence the roaring of the seas,
the roaring of their waves, the tumult of the peoples.
Those who live at earth's farthest bounds are awed by your signs;
you make the gateways of the morning and the evening shout
for joy. . . .

The pastures of the wilderness overflow,
　　the hills gird themselves with joy;
the meadows clothe themselves with flocks;
　　the valleys deck themselves with grain;
　　they shout and sing together for joy.

—————— **ALTERNATE PSALM READING: PSALM 135:5–7** ——————

(If raining, use this text)

For I know that the LORD is great;
　　our Lord is above all gods.
Whatever the LORD pleases he does,
　　in heaven and on earth,
　　in the seas and all deeps.
He it is who makes the clouds rise at the end of the earth;
　　he makes lightnings for the rain
　　and brings out the wind from his storehouses.

—————— **SILENCE** ——————

—————— **WORLD PEACE PRAYER** ——————

(Sung/prayed at noon in every time zone)

Lead us from death to life,
from falsehood to truth,
from despair to hope, from fear to trust.
Lead us from hatred to love,
from war to peace.
Let peace fill our hearts, our world, our universe.

182

─────── **BENEDICTION** ───────

Creator of heaven and earth,
who called Cuthbert from guarding sheep
in the Lammermuir Hills to be a shepherd of the people,
help us, inspired by his example, to offer friendship to all.

─────── **CLOSING PRAYER** ───────

Glory be to the Father,
And to the Son,
And to the Holy Ghost,
As it was in the beginning,
Is now, and ever shall be,
World without end.
Amen.

─────── **WALKING PRAYER** ───────

Christ behind,
Christ before,
Christ beside.

Christ below,
Christ above,
Christ within.

Source: Portions adapted from Ray Simpson, "Common Prayer from the Community of Aidan and Hilda," 446, https://www.raysimpson.org/userfiles/file/CAH_Common _Prayer__Committee_7__April_2017_updated.pdf. The World Peace Prayer was launched in 1981 by Satish Kumar and Mother Theresa in St. James's Anglican Church in Piccadilly, London, to be recited at noon in every time zone so that a continuous prayer for peace may be covering the world. The text is an adaptation of a mantra from the ancient Hindu Upanishads (800–300 BCE) and can be found in *A New Zealand Prayer Book (He Karakia Mihinare o Aotearoa)* (HarperSanFrancisco, 1997), 164, https:// anglicanprayerbook.nz. The corresponding song was created by Marty Haugen, called "Lead Us from Death to Life" (GIA Publications, 1985). Benediction from the Community of Aidan and Hilda, "St. Cuthbert's Way: Melrose to Lindisfarne—Pilgrim Prayers and Songs," https://raysimpson.org/userfiles/file/St_Cuthbert_s_Way_Pilgrim _Menu_a5.pdf. Used with permission. Midday prayer compiled by Kara K. Root.

8

Haunted by the Frame

The Church, the Kids, and the Viking Raiders

Seeking and Finding

We've crossed the border into England! As we take selfies next to a weathered wooden sign on the top of a hill with two arrows pointing in opposite directions to "Scotland" and "England," the view is beautiful in both countries. We appreciate the milestone and celebrate how far we've come. We spend a good part of today's walk high in the hills, seeing only sheep and cows amid the wispy fog and heather. Yet again, the last mile of the day is a painful struggle.

As we approach Wooler, moving from the dirt trail to the road, we happen to find ourselves walking next to Banana Split and the Three Maidens. Delirious from the walk, Kara doesn't recognize them at first. Embarrassingly, she asks one of the Maidens if they too are walking St. Cuthbert's Way, as though they're strangers. She gets the oddest look in return and holds onto the embarrassment for days. (Only Maisy is more embarrassed than Kara.)

As we enter Wooler and hit a fork in the road, Banana Split, out ahead thirty or forty feet, turns and yells back to us, "That place there," pointing his finger intensely, "has the BEST ice cream. The BEST!" The awkwardness just seems to be a common symptom of five days and fifty miles on the trail. But Maisy and Andy share a look. They wonder if Banana Split might not have an ice cream addiction, his desire for the sweet nectar taking control of his mind.

After finding our accommodations, we walk to an Italian restaurant for a delicious carb load. Pizzas, pastas, and breads fill our plates. After a few eager bites, we notice Mom and Daughter sitting across from us on the patio. It appears they've been here a while. They're surrounded by empty plates and glasses and are dealing each other cards. They're playing some game. This is a common practice in the UK and Europe that we, as Americans, just can't get used to. We eat and leave, not seeing the meal as a long invitation to sit, take in the night, enjoy the conversation. American restaurants want to optimize profits, moving people quickly so tables can be refilled, more people can be served, more money can be made. In the UK and Europe, eating is meant to be a resonant experience. To book a table is to have it for the night—if you wish. The idea is to slide in and be there, eating slowly and staying long. Hypothetically we want that, but we have been malformed by our fast food and twelve-minute school lunches.

As we get up to leave, we wave to Mom and Daughter and they gesture us over. We stand and talk for a while. They ask us how we've been finding the trail. They explain that Daughter injured her hip, so she ended up taking a taxi to Cuthbert's Cave (one of our spots on tomorrow's walk) from where we had seen them in Heathpool. From Cuthbert's Cave, they met up again and took a cab right to the Holy Island and then back here to Wooler. They've run out of time and capacity, but that hasn't dampened their experience.

They tell us that they walked St. Cuthbert's Way for two reasons. First, because of the quiet. Mom explains that there is almost nowhere else in the UK where you can be alone and in solitude like this trail in the North. She expounds that her whole body yearned for the quiet; she soaked it up like rain on dry land.

Second, Mom tells us that her stepson is from the North. The North means so much to him, she says. Her stepson even went to St. Cuthbert School. She tells us that walking the North is a way of knowing him a bit more. We get the sense that their relationship is strained. Perhaps this walk, a true pilgrimage, is a way to find him, to be connected with him, even in his absence. Mom seems to sense that by walking in her stepson's beloved North, on the trail of his saint, she might embody her

Cuthbert and King Ecgfrith

desire to be close to her stepson. Mom, as did Cuthbert, has come to the North out of a longing for connection and understanding. She's come to find a kind of relationful relating with her stepson. She is like King Ecgfrith of Northumbria long before her, who sailed into the solitude of the sea to visit Lindisfarne and Cuthbert. Like Mom, the king was looking for answers, seeking to find fruition for his desires. Mom and King Ecgfrith believe that just maybe Cuthbert can help.

187

Resonance and Desire

As we said in chapter 3, there is a shared component to St. Cuthbert's and St. Augustine's callings. For both saints, a child speaks a prophetic word that leads them deeper into faith and the calling of ministry. Augustine also never tired of reflecting on his own experiences of childhood and young adulthood. These, among other reasons, led Augustine to claim that *desire* is the central fulcrum that shapes our humanity. To quote the philosopher James K. A. Smith and his work with Augustine, "You are what you love."[1] We are what we desire. To shape children and congregations is to help aim the compasses of their hearts toward the right loves. To encourage them to desire well. To live the Christian life, Augustine believes, is to desire God. All our other desires are shaped by this desire for God.

The Christian life according to Augustine is not what you *know* or *believe*, and in some sense not even what you *do*, in contrast to the Western modern mindset. The Christian life is first and foremost what you *desire*. What is your longing pointed toward? What motivates your living and directs your life (i.e., what shapes your belief and moves your action)? What is the point? What's it all *for*?

Desire has huge ramifications for parenting and leading congregations. The job of a parent or a pastor is to shape a child's or a congregation's desires, for we are what we love. This is done not by imparting information or passing on correct knowledge—though, of course, both those things are important. Teaching those we love to love well happens more as an invitation into a particular vision of what it means to live a good life. Desire is shaped through compelling stories that spark imagination and inspire attunement to certain frequencies, orientation in certain directions. The habits we cultivate or take on without realizing, the practices we intentionally and unintentionally rehearse—and so also model to one another—are what shape our loves. As Luke

12:34 puts it, "For where your treasure is, there your heart will be also." When we love status or growth, recognition or security, progress or praise—if we desire these things because we think we'll be lost without them—that is the central desire that will inevitably shape us most deeply. Most parents want their children to be well and do well. But they fail to recognize that being well and doing well are contingent on *desiring well*. Parenting and leading congregations are first and foremost about desire.

But wait, doesn't this lead to a problem in relation to Rosa? To desire something, like Banana Split does ice cream, seems to mean we seek to possess it, to control it. Desire and passion *want* something deeply. The person overcome with passion says, "I want you" or "I want it so badly." If we desire stability or happiness or success for our children, aren't we making a third thing, beyond simply seeing and connecting with them? Even Mom walking the trail because she wants to be closer to her stepson could be seen this way. Isn't desire the drive to control?

Rosa does address the relationship between desire and uncontrollability. We cannot control what we desire. At the same time, our desires are not completely up to chance but are given to us, shaped in us, by the culture and circumstances in which we are raised. The world around us is always trying to both satisfy our desires and direct our desires toward the products and experiences that maximize profits. We live in response to our desires—making choices and taking actions that address our longings—but also the very actions we take and choices we make shape what we desire. Rosa observes two ways that desire can close us off to resonance. One way is to *always* give in to our desires, only consuming the world and thus losing ourselves. The other is to *never* give in to our desires, mooring ourselves on an ethical iceberg that keeps us unreachable by the world. Both are forms of self-alienation.

What makes a desire a desire is that it draws us out from ourselves. We cannot desire just ourselves. Desire is proof that we are beings who need otherness. Our desires pull us out to seek this otherness. But lest the desire mysteriously dissolve, that which is desired and is other than us must remain uncontrollable. As soon as we can completely grasp or control something, we no longer desire it. When we possess it or know it or master it, the I-Thou connection dissolves into I-it, we become "the very destroyer of things," and all possibility of resonance is lost. Desire is dependent on uncontrollability.

This reality of desire's uncontrollability makes pornography, for example, a poison to our children. Pornography hijacks our deepest desires, speeding us past the line of uncontrollability to make sex controllable in every way. Pornography gives us control over our bodies for our own pleasure over and over, to exercise without limit the power of our own desire. But this controllability of sex by pornography hollows out the spirit of sex itself. Sex is no longer about a desire for an encounter of uncontrollable otherness but instead becomes a capitalist commodity that is available 24/7. Desire becomes not an invitation into points of uncontrollability but an appetite that must be satisfied quickly. Pornography (and consumerism in a less titillating but equally powerful way) destroys the boundary between desire and uncontrollability. Both pornography and hyperconsumerism make what we desire controllable (i.e., visible, reachable, manageable, and usable), convenient, and always at hand. Therefore, what we desire is no longer otherness but just a flat and disappointing reflection of ourselves. Pornography is the objectification of others (I-it) in order for the self to have sex with itself (I-it). It promises *control* (leading some to wrongly call pornography "safe") but provides no *encounter*. Pornography produces optimization and kills resonance. There is no meeting of human spirit, no I-Thou that upholds and celebrates otherness, no finding fulfillment in mutual consummated uncontrollability.

Both parenting and leading congregations are about shaping desire, forming people to desire well, keeping desire linked with otherness and relationful relating. To shape our desire toward God is to shape our longings toward that which we cannot attain on our own. In our vulnerable, human inability to reach God, the uncontrollable God reaches for us. By cultivating habits of belonging and connection with one another, and by sharing semicontrollable practices of openness to God and the world, we are attuning ourselves and each other to God's presence and activity. We are making ourselves available for moments of resonance that ground us in a deeper reality than what we can manufacture for ourselves, and we are shaping our desire toward the fullness of life God offers us.

Attunement to God's Relating

A Prayer of God's Relating—Psalm 23

God is our protector and guide,
we lack nothing.
In calm beauty and safe comfort,
God rests us.
With simplicity and gentleness,
God meets our needs.
God draws our inner being back into trust
and guides our lives toward connection, honesty, and joy,
because that is who God is.
God, even when our life is at its darkest and most terrifying,
you drive out fear with love.
Your belonging claims everyone.
Where we see only barriers,
you break down hostility and widen welcome.
Continually, abundantly
you provide for our well-being.
You make us accomplices in hospitality
and drench us in blessings.
Every single day,

191

kindness, forgiveness, grace, and love
are eagerly chasing us!
Now and for all eternity,
our home is in you, Lord.
Amen.

Psalm 23: A Mad Libs Journaling Exercise

As monastic traditions have practiced for millennia, praying the psalms shapes our desire toward God as we practice relationful dialogue with the divine and reflect on God's relating with us. David was a shepherd. When he wrote Psalm 23, he used metaphors that would have been familiar to him. This "Mad Libs" journaling exercise invites you to consider what your own Psalm 23 might be.

The LORD is my _____
   (metaphor for God—e.g., shepherd)
I lack nothing.
God _____
   (ways God cares for you—e.g., "makes me lie down in green
   pastures, leads me beside still waters")
God _____
   (what needs God meets—e.g., "restores my soul")
God _____
   (way God directs and guides us, not because of what we
   deserve but because of who God is—e.g., "leads me in right
   paths for his name's sake"):
Even though _____
   (description of darkness, isolation, threat—e.g., "I walk
   through darkest valley/valley of the shadow of death")
I will fear no evil. For you are with me.
You _____
   (way God provides protection and direction—e.g., "your rod
   and your staff, they comfort me")
You _____
   (way God reconnects you to your belonging to God and all
   others, welcoming all—e.g., "you prepare a table before me
   in the presence of my enemies")

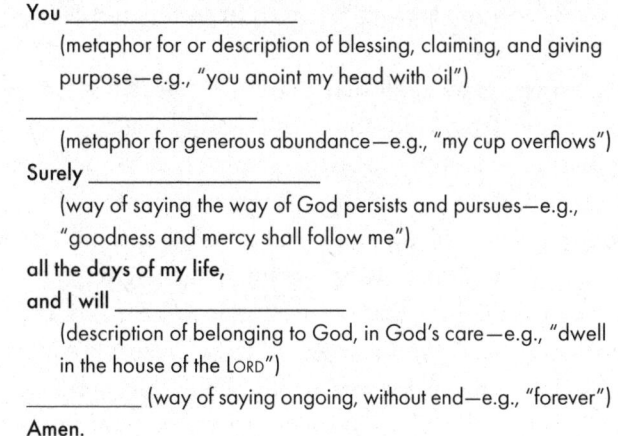

You _____
    (metaphor for or description of blessing, claiming, and giving
    purpose—e.g., "you anoint my head with oil")

_____
    (metaphor for generous abundance—e.g., "my cup overflows")
Surely _____
    (way of saying the way of God persists and pursues—e.g.,
    "goodness and mercy shall follow me")
all the days of my life,
and I will _____
    (description of belonging to God, in God's care—e.g., "dwell
    in the house of the LORD")
_____ (way of saying ongoing, without end—e.g., "forever")
Amen.

Remember, resonance requires the four components of (1) something outside ourselves reaching for us (*affected*), (2) our response or *self-efficacy*, (3) *transformation* occurring, and (4) *uncontrollability*. Desiring well means cultivating relationships with each other and the world that are reachable but not controllable. Resonance is not possible if we can't be reached by the world or we can't respond back, but resonance is also not possible if we can control others or the world. In both cases, we've lost the possibility of relationful relating, and we've lost the capacity to desire well.

So Mom's hike into the North in an attempt to reach her stepson is not necessarily a way of controlling him or dictating their relationship. Indeed, she is journeying away from him as a way to move toward him. By experiencing the world that has formed him and given him his desires, she is calibrating her own desires toward that which has shaped his heart, giving the two more points of connection and understanding. She is bringing herself into reach of her stepson. She is opening herself to resonance. Interestingly, the pursuit both of her stepson's world and also of quiet and solitude—the space to be present to herself and listen deeply to the world—is forming her for

I-Thou relating and freeing her from unseen patterns of resistance to resonance.

Eschatology plays a role here as well. We are living in a reality that is arriving from God's future but is not yet here in fullness. We may fundamentally long for and even desire (or at least desire to desire) the justice, unity, and freedom of God's vision of the good life for all humanity and creation. But the kingdom of God is neither a remote and nebulous idea completely beyond us nor something that is our responsibility to control and achieve. As soon as our desires lead us to grasp for control to make God's vision visible, reachable, achievable, and manageable, we've turned the quest for peace or the fight for justice into a project of relationless relating. We are no longer tuning our hearts to listen to God and one another. Instead, we're creating points of aggression: The world we live in becomes a problem to be solved, and the people around us obstacles to that work. We've closed ourselves off from resonant experiences of participation in God's redemption and healing. As a result, we succumb to grim predictions about the future of the world and I-it perceptions of each other. Conceptual controllability (that is, believing all things can be knowable and controllable) that causes us to be "the very destroyer of things" takes aim at hope, draining hope of its power and making it just a hypothetical idea instead of a promised future into which we are called to courageously live in trust. Trying to bring about a kingdom of God vision of a good life by means of seeking to control others or society—such as motivating people through outrage, fear, and frustration—creates more alienation, depression, and burnout. By trying to control how it happens and who gets to receive it (and who doesn't), we are actually resisting the peace and justice of God.

We can instead shape our desires toward God's kingdom by helping one another trust that God is moving the world toward redemption and healing, with us participating in that flow in obedience to, and in cooperation with, God's ongoing salvation. Rosa suggests,

> If we no longer saw the world as a point of aggression, but as a point of resonance that we approach, not with an aim of appropriating, dominating, and controlling it but with an attitude of listening and responding, an attitude oriented toward self-efficacious adaptive transformation, toward mutually responsive reachability, modernity's escalatory game would become meaningless and, more importantly, would be deprived of the psychological energy that drives it. A different world would become possible.[2]

But as long as our desires are shaped for control, we will keep approaching the world as a point of aggression. Uncontrollability is what keeps desire from becoming monstrous.

And now it is with monsters that we end our pilgrimage.

Pilgrimage, Day 6: Wooler to Fenwick

Wooler is a charming village. We sleep soundly and awaken to freshly scrubbed morning air. With the streets still damp from a predawn rainfall, we set out feeling the anticipation of closing in on our destination. This is the last long day of walking. Today we will see Cuthbert's Cave and make our way to Fenwick, our final stop before we venture tomorrow into the sea and cross to the Holy Island.

It's misty and cloudy. The cooler temperatures than yesterday are a huge relief, but visibility is low as we make our way up and down the hills, in and out of clouds. Coming down out of the hills early this morning, we stumble upon a new pilgrim who is in the final stages of cleaning up a (illegal) campsite. He hurriedly puts a large pack on his back and a small one on his front and darts out ahead before we can close the space between us. We meet up again when we reach a small village and a schoolhouse pump, where he is vigorously scrubbing his bare chest and torso with a giant sponge, craning his neck to scour under his beard. Sponge-Bath Two Packs is Italian, from Milan, and he's moving fast. He wraps up his washing, wishes us well, pulls on his rugged packs, and rapidly continues onward. We will encounter him one more time on this trip—on the Holy Island, where he arrived perhaps that same day. There we will learn he's a museum art director hosting an exhibit in Edinburgh who likes to extend his travels by tacking on (rigorous, speedy?) walks. He will point to a map of the Borderlands hanging near the abbey and declare that he's considering walking St. Aidan's Way (162 miles) before flying home to Italy. Sponge-Bath Two Packs seems to be made of different stuff than regular humans.

We pause at the pump for a more timid but equally grateful use of the water. Standing next to a bench designated for pilgrims' rest is a life-sized wooden carving of St. Cuthbert, with whom we pose for group and individual photos before moving on.

Our walk takes us through a field of cows that are *very* interested in us. An intimidating knot of them presses against a flimsy fence, leaning their faces out into our path, inches from our heads. Hearts pounding, we try to keep a steady pace and get past them quickly. Kara hums to herself to calm down, and Maisy tries not to laugh at their big nostrils flaring right next to her face.

Maisy started the day dragging but found some kind of super second wind, and for most of the day she's assuredly out ahead, confidently paving the way for the rest of us. Kara is far behind, an uncomfortable sentience emerging as she walks.

I can feel the rest of them out in front, but with the fog and mist I feel at moments like I'm walking completely alone. I pretend, off and on, that this is true. The damp air and color-saturated earth are speaking to me, and from time to time I catch up enough to the others to again see Owen's back appearing and disappearing in the cloud.

I feel acutely aware of my sin at the moment, my being trapped in defensiveness, my use of control as a coping mechanism that ends up rubbing my family the wrong way and causing division, my inability to free myself from this or even recognize I am in it much of the time. I want to leave on this trail, on the island, the me that needs to hold so tightly to my reputation or people's opinions of me, to my kids and their choices, to control in all these areas, always needing to be director of activities. I want to shed my skin and come home as the more vulnerable me that is underneath, who can let things be without having to correct or comment. I want to return freer and more available to what might be, whatever might be.

We arrive at Cuthbert's Cave, a long, shallow rock outcropping tucked in the woods about halfway to Fenwick. It's covered in carvings, people's names and dates, some from the 1800s. Cuthbert often rested in this cave, and it is also where the monks on the run with Cuthbert's body stopped and stayed. They were fleeing the monstrous, running from the experience of uncontrollability becoming demonic. The monks hid in the cave to protect themselves from the violent storm of oncoming Viking raiders. The cave covered them from an uncontrollability that sought to kill, not encounter.

Spent and touchy, an argument flares up between us, and we pull away from the kids to hash it out. They're annoyed with us for this and spend the time wandering the trails around the cave and reading the inscriptions on the cave walls. Eventually, we sort things out and the long day of walking continues.

Maisy is joyfully paving the way with unstoppable momentum. Kara remains far behind. The rest of us pause to let Kara catch up, but she's enjoying walking alone, and loving watching Maisy's confident journey, so she waves us onward. At one point a startled deer, full head of spectacular antlers, runs out onto the trail right in front of Kara, directly toward Andy. She yells out to Andy. Andy turns quickly and the frightened deer switches course and darts behind Kara, back across the path and into the woods.

Despite all of Kara's shoe-obsessing planning and control, a hideous and unwelcome blister has appeared on the baby toe of her left foot.

It's so painful that I consider quitting. "Help me let go," my morning mantra, becomes "Help me, Jesus!" in the afternoon; each step hurts so badly. Somehow, amid the pain, I decide to run, and it works! My feet land differently, and the pain is lessoned. Running with my stick held out in front of me, like the handlebar of a roller coaster, feels so ridiculous and exhilarating that it gives me energy and makes me laugh at myself. I let go of how absurd and silly I must look and just run wildly because it feels good.

Kara's outlandish trot brings her suddenly racing past the rest of us, making Maisy squeal and run faster to stay in front. And now we are all laughing, and the laughter is soothing and healing. The final mile and a half from the town of Fenwick to our inn is exhausting for all of us and excruciating on Kara's throbbing toe. Andy plays "The Eye of the Tiger" on his phone, holding it high in the air, as he and Maisy jog alongside Kara, cheering her on—and she tries to keep running through the laughter. Owen looks on tolerantly from behind, his rock-steady pace unwavering.

After dashing perilously across the A1 highway, we reach the Lindisfarne Inn. Here we cross paths again with Banana Split and the Three Maidens, who are just finishing up their ice cream. We all agree this leg was surprisingly hard. We hear more about their own reasons for walking—a married couple who are avid hikers as well as their two friends, one of whom is a novice—and some of their own joys of the journey.

We tell them good night and sit down to enjoy our dinner, finishing it off incongruously with strawberry and mint ice cream atop our sticky toffee pudding, because the restaurant had just mysteriously run out of vanilla.

Pilgrimage, Day 7: Fenwick to Holy Island of Lindisfarne

After a week of muggy weather and blazing temperatures, it is cold and drizzling when we set out the next morning. Gratefully wearing our windbreakers for the first time, we press through the wind and arrive, eager and buoyant, at the edge of the causeway. The sea has receded, leaving the mudflats exposed in low tide. We veer for the walking path—a row of thin, twenty-foot-high wooden poles sticking up from the waterlogged sand, disappearing into the distance as far as we can see—to guide pilgrims on their crossing. We step off solid ground, and Andy immediately slips on the wet rocks and lands badly on his wrist.

All of us remove our socks and shoes except for Owen, whose pace barely changes. He sets out immediately and remains well ahead of us the whole way, perhaps reaching the island twenty-five minutes before the rest of us. The sand in the shallows is slick with slime and very difficult to walk on. Kara is glad to have her walking stick along and announces it gleefully to the rest of us. We struggle forward, gingerly placing our feet. Ten minutes later the walking gets easier, the ground sandier. Owen is a mirage in the distance, marching forward with purpose.

At first we think there are millions of worms curled up everywhere, and we're nervous to step on them but find them impossible to avoid. A third of the way across we realize these are just curly piles of sand—like it had been pushed through a Play-Doh maker—from some crab or sea creature who awaits the receding tide just like the pilgrims do.

Each step in the icy water is different from the previous one. We press our feet sometimes into soft sand and sometimes into sharp shells, sometimes plunging into deep mud up to our calves—once making our way past a submerged boot with just the top lip peeking out. We slosh through ankle-deep water, dodge tangled piles of seaweed, and find the pleasant patches of soft sand again, pressing the curly piles of sand flat and leaving footprints behind us. The way is long. One hour goes by. Then another hour. Occasionally one of the tall, rugged poles marking the path has a platform attached to it, twelve feet in the air, with narrow ladder rungs leading up to it, there for the unlucky pilgrim who finds themself caught far from shore in a rapidly rising tide.[3] Maisy climbs halfway up one and waves for a photo.

Slowly and steadily, with growing confidence, we press our way through the wind, mist, and drizzle, one step at a time. It's tedious but never boring. Our calves are burning. Finally, we approach the shoreline of the Holy Island. Owen stands up from the bench he's been resting on and grins at the rest of us. We give in to the urge to whoop and holler into the wind. We've made it.

The Disillusionment of Arriving

But we are not quite finished. The pilgrimage is officially completed at the foot of the abbey ruins in the center of the island. It's only five or six hundred yards away, and yet the rest of this journey presents one final, surprising spiritual trial. One more acute reminder of uncontrollability. We feel finished, but now we must dry off our feet and legs, pull on our socks and shoes over icy toes and crusted mud, strap our wet packs onto our backs, and start up from the shoreline to join the stream of day-trippers pouring into town on the sidewalk that will dump us all onto the main street of the island.

The disconnect is jarring. We've spent a week largely in solitude, with wide swaths of silence, feeling the ground beneath us, the air around us, hearing birds and wind, attuned to our own bodies as we move, enjoying occasional conversation or singing, but focused and moving, then stopped and resting. A meal, a shower, a bed. Waking up and doing it again.

Now we approach the crowd of noisy tourists getting out of their cars and parading down the sidewalk into town with their strollers and umbrellas. We've just walked (*well over!*) sixty-three miles; they've walked sixty-three steps from their cars. And now we are in the same place. Together. As we jostle into the nearly elbow-to-elbow throng, we're surprised to find our exhilaration suddenly replaced with annoyance, tinged perhaps with a streak of righteous indignation. We're completing a journey of letting go! Must it end among people racing ahead to get T-shirts and ice cream?

Here is indeed the last temptation of the pilgrim. In 1515, young Martin Luther had a similar reaction. After walking from northern Germany to Rome, his feet aching and his spirit emptied, Luther's annoyance spikes just steps from his journey's completion. As he enters the crowded streets of Rome, Luther becomes outraged at how shabby and morally destitute the eternal city appears. It becomes one of his many proofs that the bishop of Rome is corrupt.

With the wind out of our sails and the feeling of completion behind us, the last few hundred steps are confusing and frustrating. Finally, we make it to the abbey ruins on Lindisfarne. There is no finish line to cross, no great sign announcing our arrival, nowhere to receive a badge or congratulatory toast of recognition. There is just a majestic, crumbling abbey swarming with tourists, all of it utterly indifferent to us and our great accomplishment.

We summon up weak echoes of the shoreline satisfaction, embrace our increasingly cranky children, and repeat to each other that "we did it." *We* made it sixty-three (plus!) miles. Our "we did it" hovers between us, a sure sign that we will always find it difficult to let go of control. Finishing this ancient path, we're still our modern selves. Even at the *very second* of completion, our desire to reclaim control prevails. We're struck by the necessity of the painful and important spiritual work this journey has entailed. A pilgrimage, clearly, is not a quick fix, a once-and-for-all exorcism of the incessant grasping for control. If anything, it has heightened our uncomfortable awareness of our own self-construction projects, clearly not left by the wayside as we walked but carried within us even now at the end.

Letting Go and Letting In

We leave the abbey and the crowd of selfie-taking tourists and make our way past a few enticing gift shops down a narrow lane to find our accommodations for the night. We're staying in two rooms above an old pub called The Ship Inn. It's charming and lovely, with an enormous, welcoming bathtub. Dropping our bags on the floor, propping the retired walking stick in the corner, and removing our shoes one more time, we shower off the mud and sweat and take turns having a nice long soak. We rest.

In the late afternoon we ditch the kids in their room and the two of us head back to the abbey. Entering the same streets, we find ourselves in an entirely different place. Not only have the clouds lifted and drizzle ended, but the tourists are all gone. Even the main road is empty and quiet. The crowds have hurried back across the causeway before the uncontrollable water returns. In their absence a transformation has occurred: The island's true identity is unveiled.

Suddenly what felt like a commonplace, crowded vacation destination takes on a heavy sense of wonder—a deep, still beauty. Bathed in the golden light of the late-afternoon setting sun, it's impossible not to sense that this is indeed a holy place. In the stillness of the emptied island, the ruins of the abbey stand sedate and peaceful. Without the selfie sticks and loud conversations, there is just ancient, majestic calm and a brisk sea breeze. The towering ruins reveal a silent peek into a lost world, where the human spirit yearned for, and even met, the uncontrollable Spirit of God.

Next to the abbey ruins is a small church, St. Mary's, also beautiful and haunting. At least some of the stones of this small church have lain on top of each other since 634/635. That year the Celtic monk Aiden arrived on the island to build the abbey and to create a community that sought to commune with the uncontrollable God of Israel. Aiden died here in this little church, and his spirit was accompanied by angels to heaven, as Cuthbert witnessed from his sheep watch atop the purple mountains of Eildon.

We slide into the cool, dim stone structure and make our way to the front for evening prayer. Here sit the Honeymooners, sandwiched between a dozen or so local townspeople and other overnight visitors. (Later, they will tell us that their blisters had gotten so bad they needed to taxi the last fifteen miles, which explains why we'd stopped seeing them the past couple days.) We find a spot and sit down on the antique wooden bench in the chancel, looking across at faces not unlike our own and not unlike those who have rested here to pray day after day for centuries. The setting sun streams through stained glass and puddles up in colors on the stone floor. Evening prayer begins. We chant the Holy Scriptures. We feel our spirits unclench. We are reminded again, reshaped to realize once more, that *we* didn't *do* anything. This walk was a pilgrimage, not a workout. As with the ancients who walked to, and prayed in, this little church as far back as fourteen hundred years ago, our pilgrimage was *not* about what the self can overcome and accomplish. It was a journey of release.

Framing the Church's Story

After evening prayer in Aiden's little church, our deep-seated misguidedness about the weakness or ineffectiveness of the

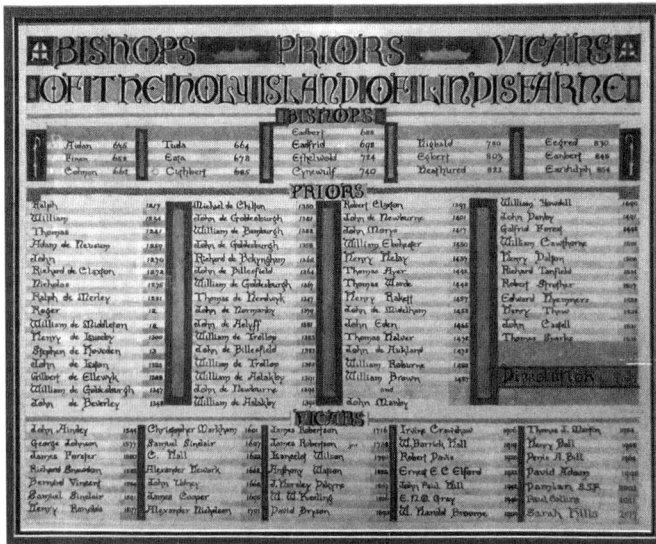

Past bishops, priors, and vicars of Lindisfarne

church, and its need to be saved by our savvy generation, sinks in for the two of us. Before leaving, we walk the perimeter of little St. Mary's inside walls, examining the art and ancient structure. On the wall closest to the sea hangs a framed, four-foot-by-two-foot calligraphed list of every bishop, prior, and vicar of this little church, going all the way back to Aiden. It's amazing to behold (especially for former youth-group stars from America!). We study it for several minutes.

At first we're struck by the continuity. Names stretch through the centuries, beginning, of course, with Aiden in 635. One after the other, all the way up to Sarah Hills, the first woman listed, who became vicar in 2019, a contemporary colleague living just down the street, carrying a chapter in a ministry in this place stretching to antiquity. We touch her name and then trace the people with our fingers, all the way to Aiden. It makes us feel small but in a way that is full. It makes things feel uncontrollable but in a way that invites. The church has a depth of wisdom that we simply cannot reach.

As we examine the picture further, we spot something else. It's something that makes sense only because we now know a bit about St. Cuthbert and see his name listed in the frame as the sixth bishop to live on the Holy Island. We notice that in the flow of continuity, from one leader to the next, there is a major gap from 854 to 1217. This more than 350 years is when the Holy Island of Lindisfarne and its church and abbey were abandoned by the faithful inhabitants because uncontrollable wind brought with it uncontrollable Viking raiders. Like the Israelites before them, the monks left and wandered from place to place, carrying Cuthbert's coffin with them. Traversing northern England, they sought a promised land in which to lay the bones of their beloved saint.

After years of wandering, the monks of Lindisfarne finally found their promised land in Durham. They laid down the bones of their saint and built one of the most beautiful and oldest of Europe's cathedrals atop them. This little church we'd just prayed in sat empty and decaying for 350 years. That's longer than the United States of America has existed as a country. We just keep repeating to ourselves "350 years? 350 years!" And yet, three and a half centuries is just a blip in the lengthy historical record before our eyes.

In our need to control the church, in our belief that good leadership is control, we often hear that this late-modern moment is *the worst of times* for the church. If we firstborn youth-group stars of megachurch lineage don't take control, using all the tools of control, the church itself will disappear. Hubris mixed with resentment leads to catastrophizing. We make proclamations that if the church doesn't change, and change fast, finding new ways to get control of our cultural situation, then the church will disintegrate into nothing.

But as we stand in this ancient church, staring at this list on the wall, it is clear to us that the church has seen harder times. It has faced moments so much more precarious than this late-modern moment. Our catastrophizing and fear of monsters is more about our own need for (and frustration with) control than it is about our openness to obeying the uncontrollable God who raised Jesus's dead body to life. As we examine the list on the wall, it seems clear to us that the church will continue with or without us—even us former youth-group stars (shocker!). The church has survived, and will continue to survive, all forms of anxious control and all monstrous uncontrollability. For, in the end and forevermore, the church is the body of the uncontrollable Son who is begotten by the uncontrollable Father through the uncontrollable Spirit.

Staring at the back wall of this ancient church, we realize that as it is with our parenting, so it is with our leadership. Our journey is about letting go for the sake of entering uncontrollability. Letting go seems the only way to enter life.

9

Door-Knocking Demons and the End of It All

The Uncontrollability of Uncontrollability

Later that evening we sit on a grassy hillside overlooking the abbey on one side and the sea on the other. The beauty and ancientness of the island feel far more accessible in the lonesome wind. Our bodies settle and we feel the journey's completion: the pain of sixty-three (actually ninety-plus!) miles in our knees and hips, and the muddled emotions in our hearts: gratitude, fatigue, descending malaise, concern over going home, and the nascent sense that something deep and indescribable has shifted within us. Taking it all in, we turn to gaze silently out at the horizon of the sea, the crumbling abbey half-walls to our backs. We reflect on the long history of the place where we sit. Beneath the beauty of this island, held sacred for thousands of years, lies deep horror, centuries-old trauma pressed into the layers of story and soil.

Throughout most of Rosa's *The Uncontrollability of the World*, he has made a case for embracing uncontrollability. But just when you feel like you've got it, ready to valorize the uncontrollable as always good, Rosa reminds us in the end that uncontrollability has its own terrible side. Rosa calls the final chapter in his book "The Monstrous Return of the Uncontrollable." The saga of this land affirms that uncontrollability can indeed be monstrous.

In 793, just decades after Cuthbert's death, marauding Vikings from across the northern sea rowed their narrow boats to the islands and then to the mainland of Northumbria, as well as for the first time to the island of Lindisfarne. They came raiding abbeys for their gold, such as the abbey we're sitting in the shadow of. Religious sites were treasure troves of precious objects, the symbolism, value, and meaning of which meant nothing more to the invaders than unguarded fortune, free for the taking. These ravenous raiders, driven by sheer, cruel, and unchecked desire, gleefully pillaged, brutally raped, and gruesomely murdered everyone who stood in their way. They came like a terrible storm moving violently across the land, and whole villages were known to flee in advance of their arrival.

When word came that the Danish invaders were again nearing Lindisfarne, the monks, taking up Cuthbert's body, hurriedly abandoned the sacred island, and with it the beloved and renowned abbey and Aiden's small church. On reaching the mainland, the monks carried Cuthbert's elaborately carved wooden coffin on their shoulders, hiding with his body for a short time in the cave we stood in a day earlier. From there, Cuthbert's body began a long nomadic period of dispensing miracles in the land. It was guarded vigilantly, sought out for healings, and even carried into battle in the late ninth century to consecrate the battlefield and bless the king's troops.

Rosa has told us uncontrollability is an essential component of resonance. You can have three elements of resonance (being reached, reaching back, and transformation), but without the fourth element, uncontrollability, there will be no resonance. But uncontrollability alone doesn't make something resonant. It can be benign or even terribly destructive. These Viking raids brought a terrifying, hellish uncontrollability to people's lives. A tornado, a hurricane, or a Viking raid brings uncontrollability without the I-Thou, only the I-it of depersonalized destruction. (Either the *I* is being bombarded by the impersonal *it* of a storm, or the Vikings' *I* is stripping the personhood of those they are maiming and killing, treating them as an *it*.) In this kind of uncontrollability, the world is not reaching toward us, we are not responding back, and the only transformation is indifferent destruction and merciless loss of life. Uncontrollability can be dangerous.

The framers and forgers of modernity sought to give us a world where the dangers of uncontrollability could be defeated through rationalized structures and operations. In response they created systems and mechanisms to control violent spasms of uncontrollability. Thankfully, it worked. Lightning rods controlled unpredictable strikes, keeping buildings from being set ablaze. Traffic lights, speed limits, seat belts, and airbags prevented senseless vehicle deaths and injuries. Breakthroughs in modern medicine gave us control over all manner of illnesses and injuries. Technology and science promised the West refuge from uncontrollability and produced in their wake a growing belief in the human ability to overcome the more malevolent impacts of uncontrollability, if not a smugness at our ability to defeat uncontrollability altogether. While this has succeeded in many ways, to assume that we've defeated uncontrollability is to miss a more looming and diabolical reality: *In the accumulation of control over so many areas of our life and world, we've created a new, monstrous uncontrollability.*

We've seen already how, by attempting to stamp out uncontrollability, we muted the dialogue—stifling the world's voice and stunting our capacity to listen and respond. But now Rosa wants to show us that gradually our very mechanisms of control—technological, social, political—have paradoxically stripped us of the control we *used to have*, thrusting us into a deeper and more menacing uncontrollability. He explains the huge chasm that now exists between what he describes as "theoretical controllability" and "practical uncontrollability." We could see this in the pandemic: As long as things are going smoothly, all our advancements seem to be making life better, but as soon as a crisis hits—shutting down the supply chain and jeopardizing those things we take for granted, such as toilet paper—life feels terrifyingly fragile and uncontrollable.

The Monsters

Rosa wants something more than just to remind us that uncontrollability is not always resonant. He argues that because of all our control, we've inadvertently produced a tragic *return* to an almost ancient kind of terrifying uncontrollability. We are back to facing the monster that is bigger than ourselves and is lurking around every corner. This time it's an uncontrollability that *we've created with all our control*, and ironically it affects the most basic human activities that should be the most straightforward—like eating, sleeping, raising children, and getting from one place to another—in ways the ancients could never have imagined. We live with anxieties like, What food *should* we eat? How much of it? How was it grown? Where was it purchased? Did my smartwatch record enough deep sleep last night? Do I have the wrong pillow for my sleeping style? Did a valve break on my CPAP machine? How much sleep medication can I take without it being dangerous?

Take traveling, for example. Through ever-increasing mechanisms of control, we've overcome the restrictions of distance with air travel. We can now fly almost anywhere. This system relies on highly specialized flight traffic control technology, meticulously coordinated human communication and cooperation that transcends linguistic, cultural, political, and geographical variations, and precisely followed timing and operating policies synced up all over the world. But a power grid failure, a sophisticated hacker, or a shortage of human agents in even just one location can shut the whole thing down, with potentially catastrophic results.

We've developed specialized software for booking a flight (or buying Taylor Swift tickets) that, if compromised, can trigger a domino of international, days-long strandings all over the world. If a massive storm hits a major hub (which is happening with ever more frequency due to climate change, which we've exacerbated with our mechanisms of control) or even if enough ground crew or flight crew become sick, now what used to be in our control—getting from here to there—is *practically uncontrollable*, even though it is *theoretically controllable*. Centuries after supposedly having learned how to control for their impact, we have returned to being menaced by things like rough weather and illness! But our world is infinitely more complicated now. Effectively removing the element of unpredictability from much of our relationship with weather actually worsened the impact of the uncontrollability. Despite being able to see trouble coming beforehand and effectively describe the impact afterward, we remain at the mercy of uncontrollable floods, forest fires, devastating heat waves, and arctic blasts. Now capricious, unexpected, invasive violence comes through our new, updated version of raiding Vikings, things like cyberterrorism, international sex-trafficking, and America's specialty: daily mass shootings, in which case we've nearly completely succumbed to uncontrollability, not even using the tools of control at our disposal, such as restrictions and laws. (And don't even get us started on AI.)

In heightened ways, unimaginable to our ancestors, we now live in ever-present anxiety. Those in the premodern world knew

211

what they could and couldn't control, making navigating the world fairly straightforward, but we now live with things that are controllable *in theory* but are completely uncontrollable *in practice*. Yet we are still supposed to behave as though we are in control! Rosa says,

> If bringing the world under control means making it manageable and predictable, then the political-social world today is becoming increasingly uncontrollable at a breathtaking pace. In the end, modernity's program of making the world controllable threatens to produce a new, radical form of uncontrollability, one that is categorically different from and worse than the original, because we are incapable of experiencing self-efficacy or establishing responsive relationships of adaptive transformation when confronted with it.[1]

Yet we continue to imagine that our only solution to this monstrous return of uncontrollability is to turn to the same technological and optimized pursuits of control that got us here in the first place. Climate change, we assume, will be solved only by capitalist innovation. A mental-health crisis produced in major part by digital isolation can be overcome by easy-to-use therapy apps. And we're convinced that the church will become irrelevant and die if we don't step up and take control of the narrative and image, if we don't redirect it toward the growth and acceleration the rest of culture is caught up in.

Resonance in Transit

As the sun sets on our pilgrimage, we feel the shift back into modern acceleration. Having moved at the three-mile-an-hour pace of the pilgrim across sixty-three (*nay, ninety-some!*) miles, our next move is to take a train to Durham. Though it is not officially part of our walking pilgrimage, we want to complete the story by visiting the cathedral and seeing the final resting place of Cuthbert before heading back to Edinburgh for our flight home. Yet the monster of practical uncontrollability is roaring. We've just learned of a countrywide train strike and are now scrambling to figure out what to do. We quickly realize that we will be stuck without the trains running. The uncontrollability creates anxiety. We just want to know how to get home! A few hours on the phone in the hotel gives us no assurance that all will be well, instead only pulling us out of the experience to point us anxiously toward the future. At the mercy of the strike, we will be fortunate to get to Durham. Once we arrive, we'll just hope our luck gets us back to Edinburgh as well. (Spoiler: to our relief, it will.) But while we wait and worry, the cathedral becomes a sanctuary from our anxiety.

We leave Lindisfarne (after rushing back to retrieve Kara's forgotten walking stick from The Ship Inn), shuttled off the island in our friend Jamie's car, taking our place amid the crush of vehicles and people in a surreal reversal of yesterday's long journey on foot. The sun is bright, the air is clean and fresh, and there seems to be no wind whatsoever. From the car's windows the pilgrim's way across the mudflats looks both magical and a lot easier than it was yesterday. Returning to the Lindisfarne Inn and calling a cab—after a short but exhausting walk along the busy freeway with all our luggage and an aborted wait for a bus—we finally end up in the train station at Berwick-upon-Tweed to travel to Durham.

Once in Durham, we get settled (and leave the kids) in our Airbnb and quickly wind our way through the shop-filled, cobblestone streets to the university and the cathedral just in time to slip into the back for evensong. The Honeymooners are here, of course (especially to see the visiting choir from Boston), and so is our Australian friend Simon! We discovered just before our trip, through his wife Brenda's Instagram, that Simon is in Durham on a writing leave, and we've arranged to meet up.

213

After the service, the three of us find a great little Turkish restaurant and have the most lovely, meandering conversation, catching up and touching base. There is something deep, enduring, and real about our friendship. We go long gaps without connecting, and then have honest and affectionate reunions. Twenty-two years ago, we wandered into Simon and Brenda's lives in Melbourne and lived alongside them for three months, when their kids were three and five. We were newlyweds, pre-kids, pre-careers, and post-trauma. We forged a kind of touchstone bond over time. Simon, a practical theologian, pastor, and former chef, is writing a book about his mom's wisdom with her recipes. It's beautiful and heart-wrenching to hear about their kids, now twenty-five and twenty-seven. We listen to how parenting keeps going, how our children never-endingly live under our skin and inside our veins—even as our role and influence wane and shift. We watch our friend both loving and letting go in this faithful dance of parenting we're finding ourselves awakening to. We're grateful for the reverberating moment of connection and the gift of wisdom from a pilgrim-friend further along the journey.

We depart the restaurant and pause on the bridge for a photo and a goodbye hug, certain we'll meet again in another city somewhere in the world several years from now, as is our pattern. Our walk back to the Airbnb has us reveling in resonance. How beautiful it is to exist in the big, wide world with people who know us in particular ways! How serendipitous to stumble upon one another a continent apart from our homes! We soak in the gratitude we feel for this evening we've shared, for Simon's sincere, gentle, perceptive presence, and for the unexpected gift he and Brenda have been in our lives.

The Monster of Durham

The next morning, after a rough night's sleep, we head into Durham for breakfast. We have now hit a wall of travel fatigue,

214

and Maisy especially needs our kids' version of the American Embassy—Starbucks. We bail on the little coffee shop we've just sat down in and head there for comfort. Afterward, Maisy and Kara take a walk to work through some tension, and they stumble upon a kind of all-purpose hardware and general shop where Kara is thrilled to discover a rubber stopper for the bottom of her walking stick. Last night she spent an embarrassing (for the kids) half hour on the outdoor steps of the Airbnb scraping her stick to make it look more finished, and this rubber stopper is her icing on the cake. (In a few days, she'll attempt to take this walking stick back with her through customs and security in the Edinburgh Airport. The kids will groan with humiliation as Kara confidently strolls through the airport with her stick. Two security guards will call over a supervisor, who will glance at the stick and exclaim, with a lilting Scottish brogue, "Well, that's really more of a *cluub* than a stick!" But he'll let it pass. Kara will be convinced it was this serendipitous rubber stopper that did the trick.)

We all reunite and head to the cathedral. Inside, we wander the impressive space, sitting for a time in prayer at Cuthbert's final resting place behind the altar. His tomb is embedded in the floor on an elevated plinth in the enormous cathedral, which was, for all intents and purposes, built around it—a majestic cathedral erected in an unlikely place to house Cuthbert's body. The town and then university sprung up around it.

We enter the old monastery to see the rest of the Cuthbert exhibit but must pause and mug for our Insta because *we are standing in the courtyard of Hogwarts!* (Amid the grandeur and legacy of a building that stretches back one and a half thousand years, it's the Harry Potter connection that makes Kara inexplicably tear up.) Our guide, seeing our delight, sneaks us off our planned course to a set of doors that, once opened, usher us into Professor McGonagall's classroom, currently being used as a dressing room for the visiting choir from Boston (never mind that it once was the chapter house where twelfth-century monks would gather for meetings).

After our Harry Potter digression, we make our way to the museum room—the old twelfth-century kitchen, with huge chimneys in the ceiling. The chimneys are now closed off and the room is temperature-controlled, filled with austere modern glass cases that hold Cuthbert's shoes (ruby slippers), his hair comb, and the striking pectoral cross he wore, now the symbol of the Durham Cathedral. (This cross was not discovered, by the way, until the 1800s, when an argument between colleagues as to its existence led one scholar to dig up the poor, oft-exhumed body of the saint—and find it much decayed indeed—with the pectoral cross embedded deep into the tissue, along with a beautiful woven stole, also now on display.)

Sanctuary from Monsters

Inside the walls of this monastery-now-museum we learn that the only way to truly defeat the monstrous is to find sanctuary inside the monstrous itself. It seems clear to us, as the last hours of our pilgrimage come to a close, that both parenting and pastoring are not about shielding our children or congregations from the monstrous but about giving them a story as a sanctuary where the monstrous is defeated by the monstrousness of the cross.

The young man who's giving us a tour of the museum looks part scholar and part comic book enthusiast. He takes us close to a glass case and asks, "Do you know what this is? Have you seen it?" He's pointing to a huge, monstrous face. Maisy jumps in, stating that she had noticed it on the front door of the cathedral. The young man explains that the one on the door is a replica and that the original, about eight hundred years old, rests behind this glass. "But what do you think it is?" he asks again.

Andy answers, "A door knocker?" He is quickly shut down, as though he said Spider-Man was DC instead of Marvel.

The young man responds, "Everyone says that, and I'm trying so hard to change people's minds. It's not a door knocker. It's called a *sanctuary ring*. See how the ring looks like legs with a pair of feet on either end? The ring is in the mouth of this terrible demon whose head is surrounded by the flames of hell, and at one time, red, jeweled eyes filled these large, empty sockets. When you grab onto the ring, you are

Sanctuary ring at Durham Cathedral

pulled from the mouth of hell. If you were being chased by the law, or fleeing for your life, if you could get to the cathedral and grab the sanctuary ring, you'd receive automatic sanctuary in the monastery. You would be kept safe here for thirty-seven days, and nobody could touch you."

Kara asks, "Why thirty-seven days?"

The guide explains that most other cathedrals use forty days, matching the years of the Israelites' wandering in the desert and Jesus's days in the wilderness. But here in Durham it's thirty-seven days because Cuthbert said so. In a dream, a prior heard Cuthbert say that thirty-seven is the number of days for sanctuary in his cathedral. And so it was that any human being who could grab the ring could find shelter inside the cathedral, inside the church's story that the monstrous act of the cross has become the transformative reality of life coming from death.

All monstrous evil has been overcome by life and love. The uncontrollable cross is the place where the monstrous uncontrollability of the world is overcome inside the deepest of encounters, the place where relationful relating is given back to

217

the world. This relationship of Jesus to us, by overcoming the monstrous, has forevermore brought us into God's own being.

Parenting and church leadership are all about the uncontrollable. We are called to invite our children and our congregations into the sanctuary of the story of the uncontrollable God who overcomes all that is monstrous by inviting us to grab hold of his own monstrous body, crucified and now resurrected and ascended. To parent and to lead in the church are to invite our beloved people to find sanctuary from the relentless tyranny of relationless relating that pursues us and demands we comply. Our job is to welcome one another back to the relationful relating that opens us to life and resonance, to walk the slow pace of love alongside God-with-us, who walks alongside us in our humanity.

We parent and lead well by aiming our desire toward life, toward connection, toward beauty and wholeness, toward the uncontrollable encounter with the wholly other divine, and the vulnerable otherness of our fellow human beings. In the midst of our fear of loss and death, we are nevertheless held by something beyond our control, called to something deeper than loss that outlasts death. We think we need to control our children's futures so they don't fall behind or fail, and we think we need to prevent our church's decline so it doesn't disappear. But these are stories that keep us from relationful relating, the outcomes of which were never in our control anyway. Parenting and church leadership are about letting go of the need for control in order to find ourselves in relationship with God and each other, to allow God to make us a sanctuary for one another.

A Journey of Trust

Pilgrims take the first step without any idea of what they'll encounter or even whether they will ever return to their regular life, which they might have considered quite controllable.

Framalicious / Shutterstock

The northern door of Durham Cathedral

If and when pilgrims return home, they cannot control *how* they will return or *who* they will be after having engaged in a drawn-out, arduous, vulnerable, and honest search for what is true. As it turns out, the purpose of a pilgrimage is to let go of all illusions that we have any ability to control any part of the world whatsoever. A pilgrimage is an intentional movement of recognizing and confessing that we have no control and that our only hope is the uncontrollable God of the uncontrollable cross.

Death is the great uncontrollability toward which every life leads. In the face of that, in the very midst of that, on this mortal journey, we are not alone. We are guided by and held in God's love in the church—the collection of sanctuary-sharing fellow pilgrims who came before us and will come after us, reaching wider, deeper, and longer than our own short and limited stints on this fragile island earth in a vast and uncontrollable universe. The church is our mother. And until the kingdom comes in its fullness, the church is fit to hold us in her uncontrollable embrace.

NIGHT PRAYER

In the name of the sending Father,
in the name of the pilgrim Son,
in the name of the wind-like Spirit,
in the name of the Three in One.
Amen.

CALL TO WORSHIP

Let the sun go down and the earth become still,
and let the Son of God draw near.
In the darkness we can see the splendor of the universe—
blankets of stars, the solitary glowing of planets.
In the darkness the wise three found the star that led them to
  you.
In the darkness of dreams you speak to your people.
As the day begins to fade, let the treasures of dark draw near.

PSALM READING: PSALM 139:1–10

O LORD, you have searched me and known me.
You know when I sit down and when I rise up;
  you discern my thoughts from far away.
You search out my path and my lying down
  and are acquainted with all my ways.
Even before a word is on my tongue,
  O LORD, you know it completely.

You hem me in, behind and before,
and lay your hand upon me.
Such knowledge is too wonderful for me;
it is so high that I cannot attain it.

Where can I go from your spirit?
Or where can I flee from your presence?
If I ascend to heaven, you are there;
if I make my bed in Sheol, you are there.
If I take the wings of the morning
and settle at the farthest limits of the sea,
even there your hand shall lead me,
and your right hand shall hold me fast.

BENEDICTION (DRAWN FROM EPHESIANS 3:17–19)

May Christ dwell in your hearts through faith, that you—being rooted and grounded in love—may have the power to comprehend, with all the saints, what is the breadth and length and height and depth, and to know the love of Christ that surpasses knowledge, so that you may be filled with all the fullness of God.

CLOSING PRAYER

Awake, may we watch with Christ.
Asleep, may we rest in peace.
The grace of our Lord Jesus Christ,
the love of God,
and the fellowship
of the Holy Spirit
be with us all.
Amen.

——— RESTING PRAYER ———

Christ behind,
Christ before,
Christ beside.

Christ below,
Christ above,
Christ within.

Source: Call to worship and portion of closing prayer from the Community of Aidan and Hilda, "St. Cuthbert's Way: Melrose to Lindisfarne—Pilgrim Prayers and Songs," https://raysimpson.org/userfiles/file/St_Cuthbert_s_Way_Pilgrim _Menu_a5.pdf. Used with permission. Night prayer compiled by Kara K. Root.

Epilogue

And Then...

Back at the Durham train station, we are celebrating that our train is going to Edinburgh after all and that we'll make our flight. We are tired and ready to go home. By all accounts, this trip feels like a success.

This is the moment we discover that Maisy's brand-new $400 retainer is missing. It's been lost today somewhere in Durham. We open her bags on a train platform bench and frantically paw through everything. It's clearly gone. There is no time to search for it; there is no next train to take. Andy's patience has vanished, and he's holding Kara back from taking a quick mile dash back to the lunch restaurant just to check.

The ancients would marvel at our anxiety. Imagine if they could see how the long arm of control reaches even into our mouths, to push and pull and hold our teeth just so, and then the monster of uncontrollability sends us into a crazed flurry of regret and stress when we lose this tiny plastic implement of control.

We feel it. Just when we think this lesson of letting go has landed inside us and we are ready to embrace the uncontrollable, everything in us wants control back. We'd like to make a world where things are never lost, where time can be turned back, where money isn't wasted. We're spinning in our own regret-filled irritation (How could we have neglected to put her name and phone number on the case?) and fruitless problem-solving (Could we find the phone numbers of where we've been? Where would we even look? Would it matter if we don't have time to go back there anyway?).

Here in front of us is the daughter we love, swamped in her own regret and struggle for control, taking on the brunt of our frustrated need for control.

A year from now, we will look back on this pilgrimage and find ourselves freshly learning something about loving and letting go. The Greek word we translate as "forgive" means simply "to let go." In not too long we will be dropping off Owen at college many states away, feeling the shock that after eighteen years of raising a person, looking out for them and looking after them, we just send them away to fend for themselves and that's that. Of course, we know that's not that and all that, but still there's *a lot* of letting go involved. There's an uncomfortable surrender that makes life feel precarious and precious all at once. And how similar the captivity of regret and fear can feel! Not unlike anger, resentment, harbored pain, or the obstinate need to be right. We can be trapped by it. How much our worry can keep us from being present in love to those we love! All of it ties us up and keeps us chained.

But in our learning to let go there *is* a kind of fundamental *forgiveness* to it all, a gentleness with ourselves, a grace for each other, an acceptance of life as it is. We will discover, with our kid on the other side of the country navigating his own brand-new adulthood, that his childhood, and our family life as it was, will have ended, and something new will be taking shape.

The truth is none of us can go back and do anything differently, and none of us can control what will happen in the future. In a moment of frustration or transition, these two facts could paralyze us with sorrow or anxiety. But we are forgiven. And we can forgive—which is to say, we are released from keeping score, and we can be free from illusions of control.

Letting go, of course, allows in the sorrow, fear, loneliness, or absence of a moment, but it also opens us to the delight, wonder, connection, and presence in the present. All of these can be doorways to resonance. Letting go attunes us again to the incredible privilege it is to love, and the awe we feel at being loved by these particular, quirky, and astonishing humans our lives are tangled up with. When we let go, we find ourselves unclenching. In the same way, letting in all that love and gratitude can help us to let go, help us to forgive. We discover we are being set free (free for) to receive the unearned, undeserved gift of each of our one, limited life, bound inextricably to the dear people we can love only by letting go.

Instead of being caught in regret over what happened or didn't happen, or paralyzed in fear and anxiety over what might or might not be, we can live right now, alongside each other, in the very presence of the living God who is right here with us. Instead of grasping for control we will never have or security we will never reach, we can let go and find we are already held secure by love.

What if the journey of a pilgrim is a constant journey of forgiveness? One step, then another, forgiving the capricious universe, forgiving our limited selves, forgiving our imperfect fellow pilgrims. Moving through the world soaking in the forgiveness of God, doling out forgiveness gratuitously and unreasonably, refusing to keep score, undermining the deception of control, choosing instead presence, vulnerability, hope. Choosing to trust that God indeed holds the universe in God's loving grasp, and the church itself—we, you, and us, all who have gone before in our faith tradition and all who share Christ's mark in this wide world—is merely a vast collection of seeking-to-be-conscious recipients and longing-to-be-available conduits of a kind of essential joy that humans encounter and share when we give up grasping and simply receive.

We are human beings all, caught together in the push and pull but also sharing together in a life filled with the possibility of touching transcendence at any unexpected moment. The spiritual journey of letting go never ends.

In the Durham train station, we finally pause the panic and see one another. Some tears, some words, some choices to release the regret and accept what is, and we're back on track. We find our seats on the train back to Edinburgh and depart the station, leaving the retainer behind and forgiving ourselves for it.

From the speed of our perch on the tracks the world blurs into a pretty picture, pleasantly removed and easily overlooked as it whips by the thick windows of our high-speed, Wi-Fi-enhanced, air-conditioned train car. Except now we find ourselves gazing out—across vast fields of golden straw, with their giant symmetrical hay bales dotting all the way to the horizon, the undulating hills with strips of dark green forest nestled between them, and it's not just a picture. We can feel it in our feet: that cool, needle-strewn forest floor. The thick, padded-down trails of fallen wheat that crunches beneath us as we find the narrow way winding alongside the tidy rows of planted crops, the path hidden from us here, at this distance and pace. We can smell the earthy pine forests, the pungent dung piles, the damp early morning mist, and the heat of the sun baking the ancient mossy rock walls that drape miraculously like ribbons over hills all across the countryside. Looking out at a flock of sheep, we can almost hear the tinkling bells and gentle baaing that alerted us to their presence, hidden in the fog and scattered among the purple heather. We look out the window, and the world is not the same. This view from this train is not the same view as it was a week ago. We are not the same as we were then.

We catch each other's eyes, and a small smile passes between us. Then we put our earbuds back in, we pick up our book and iPad, and our attention is taken away once more from this moment, away from the slow, steady world that's racing by our window.

Notes

Chapter 1 Control-Freak Parenting

1. Greg Lukianoff and Jonathan Haidt, *The Coddling of the American Mind: How Good Intentions and Bad Ideas Are Setting Up a Generation for Failure* (Penguin, 2019).

2. Many of us have just abandoned the church. It's not worth the anxiety or the effort—she's too far gone. Who wants to be stuck babysitting a declining, irrelevant, and dying institution whose time is over? Especially when making the message palatable and applicable to our lives requires so much mental contortion and energy, and when listening to outdated stories, or learning passé practices, demands so much time and patience. Not to mention, we get very little immediate fulfillment from the investment—who has the bandwidth to invest limited attention, energy, and time into fixing what's clearly broken and undoubtedly on its way out anyway? Better to reclaim our Sunday mornings for more productive activities.

3. Benjamin Franklin, "Advice to a Young Tradesman," July 21, 1748, printed in George Fisher, *The American Instructor: or Young Man's Best Companion. . . . The Ninth Edition Revised and Corrected* (Philadelphia: Printed by B. Franklin and D. Hall, at the New-Printing-Office, in Market-Street, 1748), 375–77, available at https://founders.archives.gov/documents/Franklin/01-03-02-0130.

4. Hartmut Rosa, *The Uncontrollability of the World* (Polity, 2020), 30.

5. Mark Buchanan unpacks this beautifully in *God Walk: Moving at the Speed of Your Soul* (Zondervan, 2020).

6. Theologian Kosuke Koyama contends that love has a speed, and it's slow. Jesus Christ, God-with-us, accompanies us in love at the human walking speed of three miles an hour. Koyama, *Three Mile an Hour God: Biblical Reflections* (Orbis, 1979).

Chapter 2 The Thrill of Uncontrollability

1. US Department of State, "2023 Report on International Religious Freedom: United Kingdom," https://www.state.gov/reports/2023-report-on -international-religious-freedom/united-kingdom.
2. Hartmut Rosa, *The Uncontrollability of the World* (Polity, 2020), 1.

Chapter 3 Get Aggressive, Get, Get Aggressive

1. Boisil likely takes his name from the Eastern Cappadocian theologian and bishop Basil of Caesarea. Basil is best known for his theological genius in relation to working out the confession of the Trinity. With his brother and his best friend (the two Gregorys), Basil defended and deepened the Nicene Creed's commitment that Jesus was true God of true God, begotten but not made. Basil is less famous for his pastoral and organizational genius, but it was Basil in the East who set monastic life on faithful footing. It makes good sense that a young prior in the West would take a version of his name.

Chapter 4 Grow, Grow, Grow

1. Hartmut Rosa, *The Uncontrollability of the World* (Polity, 2020), 9.
2. Rosa, *Uncontrollability of the World*, 9.
3. Rosa, *Uncontrollability of the World*, 9.
4. Rosa, *Uncontrollability of the World*, 15.

Chapter 6 The Longest Mile

1. Hartmut Rosa, *The Uncontrollability of the World* (Polity, 2020), 30.
2. Rosa, *Uncontrollability of the World*, 31.
3. Rosa, *Uncontrollability of the World*, 32.
4. Rosa, *Uncontrollability of the World*, 38.

Chapter 7 Losing What We Never Had

1. Hartmut Rosa, *The Uncontrollability of the World* (Polity, 2020), 41.
2. Rosa, *Uncontrollability of the World*, 44.
3. Rosa, *Uncontrollability of the World*, 45.
4. Rosa, *Uncontrollability of the World*, 59.
5. Rosa, *Uncontrollability of the World*, 56.
6. Thanks to Arlene Flancher for this observation.
7. Rosa, *Uncontrollability of the World*, 80.
8. Rosa, *Uncontrollability of the World*, 88.
9. Rosa, *Uncontrollability of the World*, 90.
10. Scott Evan Davis (@scottevandavis), "These weeks are too long," TikTok, January 13, 2023, https://www.tiktok.com/@scottevandavis /video/7188254738259938602.
11. Rosa, *Uncontrollability of the World*, 93.

12. Rosa, *Uncontrollability of the World*, 95.
13. Rosa, *Uncontrollability of the World*, 97.
14. Rainer Maria Rilke, quoted in Rosa, *Uncontrollability of the World*, 98.

Chapter 8 Haunted by the Frame

1. James K. A. Smith, *You Are What You Love: The Spiritual Power of Habit* (Brazos, 2016).
2. Hartmut Rosa, *The Uncontrollability of the World* (Polity, 2020), 108.
3. Rumor has it that if you get trapped in the rising tide and find yourself stranded safely atop one of these platforms, you can get rescued by boat for a hefty, quadruple-digit fee, or you can hunker down and wait out the night. The choice is yours!

Chapter 9 Door-Knocking Demons and the End of It All

1. Hartmut Rosa, *The Uncontrollability of the World* (Polity, 2020), 114–15.